MYTHMAKING

Heal Your Past
Claim Your Future

Marilyn –
What a wonderful adventure
this has been. I have
such deep respect for you,
as a woman and writer.
Thank you –
    Patty

MYTHMAKING

Heal Your Past
Claim Your Future

Patricia Montgomery, Ph.D.

SIBYL
PUBLICATIONS

Portland, Oregon

Published by SIBYL Publications • a division of Micro One, Inc.
123 N.E. Third Avenue, Suite 502 • Portland, Oregon 97232

Copyright © 1994 Sibyl Publications

All rights reserved. No part of this book may be reproduced without permission from the publisher, except by a reviewer who may quote brief passages in a review; nor may any part of this book be reproduced, stored in a retrieval system, or copied by mechanical photocopying, recording, or other means without permission of the publisher.

Consulting Editor: Marilyn McFarlane

Graphic Design: Design Studio Selby

6 5 4 3 2 1

Credit is given to HarperCollins Publishers, Inc. and Dr. Bolen for the quote and discussion from *Goddesses in Everywoman* by Jean Shinoda Bolen, Copyright © 1984 by Jean Shinoda Bolen, M.D.

Library of Congress Cataloging in Publication Data
Montgomery, Patricia D.
    Mythmaking : heal your past, claim your future / Patricia
    Montgomery.
        p. cm.
    Includes bibliographical references.
    ISBN 0-9638327-3-5

    1. Women—Psychology. 2. Mythology. 3. Self-realization. I.
Title.
HQ1206.M66 1994   305.42
                                         QB194-21094

Printed and bound in the United States of America

This book is dedicated to the women in my college classes who are role models and companions for each other. I find their vulnerability, courage, and willingness to take risks breathtaking.

Contents

Foreword

s many people recognize, we are at a turning point in history. Two powerful forces newly shape our vision as we move toward the next millennium. One is the probability of a major planetary crisis, the origin of which may be disease or environmental catastrophe or human conflict. The other is the recent wave of feminism that has brought about new ways of seeing, thinking, speaking—whole new worlds. These major influences are wakening us to the fact that we need new stories to live by. The old ones no longer work.

The old stories are about power-over: conquest, mastery, and dominion over others, ourselves, the earth. In them we witness heroic quests, wars and antagonism between people, or the subordination of some peoples or natural resources and animals to other people. The old stories get us into trouble, at this moment when our natural resources are nearly depleted, women and men dream of equal partnership, and oppressed peoples are recovering voice and action. We need new stories that weave a narrative of coo*peration, limitation,* and *equality of influence.*

MYTHMAKING has given us a treasure of just such new stories. These are imaginative narratives written by women of all ages and backgrounds who have found themselves in the classes of Dr. Patricia Montgomery. In finding themselves they have cast a wide creative net in which each reader will also find herself. There is something here for everyone. Animal stories, sci-fi, new myths, social commentary (for example, on the "creation of PMS"), and adventure stories of every type. Women's emotions of self-discovery are the underpinnings: joy, rage, enthusiasm, curiosity, grief, anger, jealousy, love, attachment, anxiety—but little aggression, hatred, envy. The relationship between reader and story stirs images of self-discovery and a new intimacy (based on equality and mutuality). Each reader will discover and uncover her own images as she or he resonates with the dreams, fantasies and imagination of the authors.

In the introductory chapters, Dr. Montgomery tells us how and why myth is important to our development. She invites each of us to discover our own stories and to follow the process, set out step by step, that the authors followed in composing their lives as story. This kind of writing is not so much therapy as it is celebration. I hope that all of us can celebrate these stories by writing our own, by sharing our stories with others, because the world needs new stories that offer plot and characters to move us way beyond the old versions of "Happily ever after ... " in which the Princess married the Prince, and she stayed at home while he went on to conquer. Neither staying at home nor conquering will lead us into the future of partnership and community that the next millennium will demand of us, if we can change fast enough to continue on this planet.

As a Jungian analyst and a feminist, I feel privileged to have a brief word here among these funny, sad, feisty tales. My world has been enriched in reading them and having the pleasure of seeing into the hearts of those women who've offered them. I welcome you, dear reader, to these stories for a new world.

— POLLY YOUNG-EISENDRATH, PH.D.
Jungian Analyst and Psychologist
Burlington, Vermont

Long afterward, Oedipus, old and blinded, walked the roads. He smelled a familiar smell. It was the Sphinx. Oedipus said, "I want to ask one question. Why didn't I recognize my mother?"

"You gave the wrong answer," said the Sphinx.

"But that was what made everything possible," said Oedipus.

"No," she said. "When I asked, What walks on four legs in the morning, two at noon, and three in the evening, you answered, Man. You didn't say anything about woman."

"When you say Man," said Oedipus, "you include women too. Everyone knows that."

She said, "That's what you think."

MURIEL RUKEYSER
Breaking Open

Introduction

The Power
of Story

Stories shape our lives. When we were young girls, many of us devoured the old myths, legends, and fairy tales. We searched for stories that would inspire and guide us into adulthood. We loved Cinderella, Beauty and the Beast, Snow White and the Seven Dwarfs, and all the others that not only entertained us but defined our roles and expectations. The stories were threads that connected us to the images, to the culture we share, and to each other.

At midlife, when we get together with women friends, we still find ourselves instinctively connecting through stories. We tell each other tales of childhood and adolescent experiences, we share current anecdotes, and we talk about the patterns that have formed through the years. Telling personal stories can be profoundly moving and meaningful, and to hear another woman's story is often inspiring.

In an earlier day, families and communities gathered to hear stories that passed on traditions and values and provided community identity. Women's lives were generally based on the expectations of their parents and their parents before them, expectations expressed in stories that usually carried a single theme: find your prince and live happily ever after.

Myths are tales that explain the meaning and goals of our lives. In the late twentieth century, we are finding that former myths no longer apply and old methods of living are outdated and unusable. The stories that may have provided guidance and comfort in generations past do not help us to deal with the massive changes and the seeming chaos in our culture. We need new myths.

Stories in a Changing Society

Today, stories are emerging that offer exciting new perspectives; they reflect and are relevant to women's changing lives.

Often, when we go through a crisis, we turn to the stories of contemporary women to show us how to cope, to survive, and to prevail. We are hungry for the stories that reveal our strength and our wisdom, that teach us how to be the heroes on life's journey, rather than the victims. And after we hear the stories and recognize our common struggles and goals, it's with a deep sense of relief that we discover we are not alone on the path.

Many of these new myths have a sacred dimension. As we share them with others, we find that we experience not only a strong sense of ourselves and our places in the world, but we connect with something greater than ourselves—a universal energy. We learn, finally, that there is healing and transformative power in myth, symbol, and metaphor. But we cannot know that power until we tell our stories.

Personal Stories as Myth

I discovered the transformative power of storytelling in 1986 when, as part of my doctoral research, I interviewed women who were undergoing midlife career change. I had a very personal interest in midlife change; at the age of 52 I had left my home and a tenured teaching career to move to another state and pursue a doctoral degree.

For the research, my interview question was, "What was the critical event or crisis point that led to a dramatic midlife career change?" The experience of telling her story was profoundly moving for each of the women I interviewed. Several spoke of being a "heroine" on life's journey. As a result of the responses, I began to look for literature that would shed light on the power of stories and myths for women. I also began to see the midlife years—usually beginning somewhere in the mid-thirties—as a period when we pursue a deeper *inner* sense of ourselves.

This led me to design college classes for women that allowed time for stories to emerge in written and oral form, as well as through creative projects. The power of my classes stemmed from women sharing their stories and then finding meaning in the themes that emerged. Something magical happened. The process and the sharing validated their life experiences, struggles, and questions and gave each of them a focus as they faced current dilemmas and decisions in their lives.

I was stunned by the impact on the other students as I read some of the stories aloud in succeeding classes. Emotional responses included relief, surprise, sadness, pleasure, as each listener identified with some aspect of the story. One story in particular, "The Lost Purr," generated strong reactions: silence, at first, and then an emotional outburst, "This is my life!" The listeners felt that part of them, their "purr," was lost somehow in the tug and pull of daily living and accommodating others.

We begin to heal through our stories. Because my goal as a teacher is to promote healing and transformative change for women, I was confident that a book containing these stories could also contribute to the shaping of a new cultural mythology for women.

Rollo May, the great psychologist, says, "A myth is a way of making sense in a senseless world. ... Myths are like the beams in a house: not exposed to outside view, they are the structure which holds the house together so people can live in it." This is what we're looking for today—structures that will hold our houses together.

This book explores the process of building such structures, as we discover the myths, messages, and stories that shape us. By perceiving the meaning behind our choices and actions, we reveal patterns that we may see as limiting, unfulfilling, and in need of change. Story-making can open new paths.

The intent is to inspire you to examine your own life patterns so that you may write the myth of your life. In that process, you may awaken to parts of yourself that are waiting to be expressed. Your discoveries may lead you to make different choices in life, or they may not. Either way, you will find yourself with a new perspective on the meaning of your life.

Thirty of the myths told here in Part 2 were written as creative writing assignments in my college classes. The authors were women, ranging in age from 23 to 63, who were undergoing some type of personal change or transition. In their stories they explored their own lives, searching for the underlying meanings and patterns. Writing the stories was challenging and sometimes difficult, they said, but always rewarding.

After creating their myths, the women made such comments as:

"Writing my own personal fairy tale was a very moving and powerful experience. When I was done, I read it to my husband and I cried. I feel something special happened to me during the process of recall and writing."

"I didn't realize until now that I really expected to live 'happily ever after,' and I didn't want to admit that it wasn't happening."

"This has been a very affirming experience for me, as well as enjoyable. The ability to 'name it' and 'claim it' applies to both the negative and positive

aspects that I would like to clarify in my life."

"No wonder! My life has been so difficult, but I always thought it was because there was some-thing wrong with me. Now I realize I've lived my life according to old myths that don't work for me."

It's my hope that these stories, along with the process of writing your myth, will empower you to take charge of your life. In changing yourself, you will join others in changing the world.

— PATRICIA MONTGOMERY

PART 1: THE POWER OF MYTHMAKING

Chapter 1: Why Women Need New Myths

The Power of Myth

T he English word myth is derived from the Greek word *mythos*, meaning word or story. Myths are narrative patterns that give meaning to our lives. Sam Keen, author of *Your Mythic Journey*, describes myth as "interlocking stories, rituals, rites, customs and beliefs that give a pivotal sense of meaning and direction to a person, a family, a community, or a culture." In other words, myth is a belief system that sustains us.

Our culture has all kinds of strong, often unspoken, generally accepted beliefs that shape our lives and dictate our behavior. One of our cultural beliefs, for example, is, "All people in our society are free." In reality, some have much more freedom than others. One group (white males) has long dominated other groups (women and minorities) and had a free rein. The theme of domination and subordination is pervasive in many of the old tales. Women's presumed dependency, the expectation that we will care for others at our own expense, and our culture's denigration of "strong" women preserve women's second-class status.

Now the myth gap is beginning to close. With the growth of the women's movement and other societal changes, we're creating new myths and new ways of living that offer visions of equality. As our lives change, so do our myths. We share our stories, and new cultural myths emerge to guide us as well as future generations.

"That's a myth," we hear women say when referring to outworn social customs and beliefs. The women in my classes say they are finding that the myths of previous generations, even their mothers' myths, no longer work for them. They seem irrelevant and even harmful. Their meanings constrained us as girls, preventing us from becoming all we can be as adults.

Themes in the outdated myths that were passed on to many women are those of self-sacrifice, dependency, and devaluation of personhood. They're revealed in these messages:

A good mother sacrifices herself for her children.

A happy family is the "Beaver Cleaver" family.

Women are to be helpmates to their husbands.

Girls are to be seen and not heard.

Nice girls never get angry.

If you're too smart, the boys won't like you.

Be careful.

You don't really feel that way.

Think back to when you were a little girl. What were your hopes and dreams? What did you think was possible? Did you believe you could be anything you wanted to be? Did you assume your destiny was to grow up, get married, and have a family? What messages were you given about how to lead your life?

Absorbing these childhood messages and living a life according to old myths is deadening and constricting for women today. Again and again, I see women chafing at the boundaries, unwilling to sacrifice some part of their nature in order to conform to expectations. Some of us rebelled to break out of the limiting world that lingers on as women's legacy. Some of us, realizing that our lives have been governed by unwanted messages, started to examine our stories, looking for what worked, what was missing, and what needed to be changed. We discovered messages that were instilled in us, unknowingly and unconsciously, about who we were and how we are to live. Many of us, until the women's movement opened different options and new stories, followed traditional paths. Now we are seeking those less trodden. We're all breaking new ground.

The famed anthropologist Joseph Campbell stated, "There are no models in our mythology for an individual woman's quest. Nor is there any model for the male in marriage to an individuated female." It's up to us. Unless we become conscious of our personal myths and are willing to change them and thus redirect our futures, we remain dominated by the old ones.

We each find a storyline that describes our life structure. It reveals the underlying pattern, with all the role models, groups, organizations, objects, and places that shaped us. This is our life design.

When we begin to understand our own stories, we learn how the past has shaped us, and at that moment we find that we can break free. The past no longer holds us prisoner, and we can create a future based on thoughtfully chosen values, goals, and ideals. Sam Keen says wisely: "We need to reinvent ourselves, remembering our past, revising our future, reauthorizing the myth by which we live."

In my teaching and counseling work, I have found that many women feel that they *are* reinventing their lives, seeking unfamiliar paths. These are the women who have broken with tradition. They're forging careers in traditionally male professions; returning to college later, in search of themselves; struggling with depression, low self-esteem, and abusive relationships. They have moved out of victimhood and are taking action, as they envision daring possibilities. These are women who have moved beyond *surviving* to *thriving*.

Creating a New Mythology

An integral part of reclaiming our power as women is acknowledging the new women's mythology and ourselves as mythmakers. Bookstores today are full of inspiring stories of contemporary women telling about the hard work, realities, and truths of their lives. These are the stories we long to hear. They reveal women who are heroes, who courageously overcome great odds, pain, and despair to find their own power and authenticity. They offer exciting new perspectives; they reflect and are relevant to women's changing lives.

We are also rediscovering the ancient myths that connect us to our heritage of strength and beauty. Clarissa Pinkola Estés' book, *Women Who Run with the Wolves,* is rich in storytelling and full of timeless myths from ancient cultures that honored powerful women. She found that women's oral traditions—the passing on of teaching tales about "sex, love, money, marriage, birthing, death, and transformation"—were lost. Many fairy tales and myths that reveal women's mysteries and power were distorted to suit a male-dominated culture. In their revision we lost the power of our "motherline"—the linear ancestral heritage of women who have gone on before us, in all of their wisdom and strength.

Beyond the personal realm, women are searching for myths that connect them with each other and with the community. One of the most powerful things to happen in my women's classes is the bonding. It deepens as we come together week after week. In small groups, we learn to appreciate and value our differences and share in the creation of new stories.

As we foresee a world rich in possibilities, we begin to take the first steps together toward achieving our vision. In creating a personal mythology through our own healing work, we begin to create a cultural mythology in which women *are* equal, in which women are potential heroes in the renewal of society.

Chapter 2: Archetypal Female Themes

Ancient Myths

Ancient myths live on in the stories we tell about our lives. Within them lie the characters and the themes of ancient archetypes and old myths. In creating our myths, we may thread together a dozen or more stories that explain our lives. In this way we create a mythology that explains the basic questions of life: who we are, what we are doing, and why.

At various times in our lives, our desires and behaviors may be dominated by different *archetypes.* An archetype is a powerful inner force or pattern, as opposed to a *stereotype,* which is an outside force, the role society expects us to play. Jean Shinoda Bolen, the author of *Goddesses in Everywoman,* sees women "acted on from within by goddess archetypes and from without by cultural stereotypes."

Bolen uses female archetypes in the form of Greek goddesses to explain the psychological quest for wholeness and individuation. The goddesses represent various traits that are responsible for major differences among women. By identifying these archetypes and bringing them to the conscious level, we can make use of the gifts and strengths that each symbolizes. We can also choose to allow other archetypes, or goddesses, to guide us.

Bolen suggests that we continually encounter moments of decision, nodal points that decide events or alter character. If a woman's behavior is consistent with her values, she is meeting her potential as the hero-protagonist of her own myth. She is a choice-maker rather than a victim, and when she feels the need she can shift from one emphasis, or goddess pattern, to another.

Midlife is often the time when a woman-hero chooses to make the shift as she follows her quest for self-discovery. She may find, lose, and rediscover what has the deepest meaning to her, holding on to her values under all kinds of circumstances. Many of the stories in this book reflect this quest. A woman on this cyclical journey experiences difficult times but gains consciousness and wisdom, finally finding harmony and peace.

Bolen identifies seven goddess archetypes. The Virgin Goddesses—Artemis, Athena, and Hestia—are independent, self-sufficient, not victimized, and not distracted from their purpose. They expand the current notion of feminine attributes to include competency and self-sufficiency.

Hera, Demeter, and Persephone are labeled the Vulnerable Goddesses and carry the traditional roles of wife, mother, and daughter. These are the archetypes whose identities and well-being depend on being in a relationship and are the roles that many of today's midlife women were socialized to fulfill.

The seventh Goddess, Aphrodite, or Venus, is more balanced. She somehow maintains her autonomy, balancing both masculine and feminine qualities. She is neither fiercely independent nor dependent, but interdependent. Many women who are divorced after long marriages feel the strong pull of Aphrodite as they explore their sexuality in new ways.

You may find any of these goddesses reflected in you. Consider Hestia, the Goddess of the Hearth, the keeper of the home. Are there periods of time when you rearrange your furniture, enjoy putting on dinner parties, create a space for your artistic projects? This is Hestia manifesting herself.

What about the years when Hera ruled, those years when you devoted your time and energy to your family, perhaps neglecting yourself? Artemis, the Goddess of Hunt and the Moon, finds the wilderness her domain. Have you longed to be out in nature for exploring, for grounding, or seeking consolation? Your inner Artemis is urging you on.

The power of these archetypes is their ability to give us perspective on our behavior patterns and personality traits. They also help us to call upon needed strengths and qualities within ourselves. One student found that Athena energy was essential when she returned to college at age 46. Knowing this, she was able to de-emphasize the roles of Hera (marriage and wife) and Demeter (mother) in order to focus on studies. Needless to say, changing roles may be hard on one's family!

In my own life story, I found that I lived the roles sequentially: first, as a 1950s mother, in the suburbs with five children in nine years. I was a superb Hera and Hestia. Later, Persephone, the dutiful daughter, was pre-eminent. That role, limiting and constricting, eventually affected my health. When my husband and I divorced after 25 years of marriage, I experienced my Aphrodite phase. Three years later, I called upon the energies of Athena as I entered graduate school. During the past two years, Artemis has emerged, demanding more time in nature, particularly the mountains. Now I see myself incorporating qualities of all of these archetypal energies to become more whole as a human being.

For a woman at midlife, a temporary withdrawal from the outer world and into inner exploration is essential. She must go into a place of silent waiting for her creative deliverance. In an ancient archetypal Sumerian myth, Inanna, Goddess of Heaven and Earth, descends to the underworld and eventually returns. This story symbolizes the withdrawal and return that is revealed both in women's psychology and in the cycles of nature. Withdrawal is seen as a time of isolation and introspection, which may lead to deeper insight.

Sylvia Perera, in her book *Descent to the Goddess*, suggests four perspectives on the ancient myth of Inanna. She says that the myth refers to the seasons and rhythmic order of nature, the initiation into the mysteries of the self, the process of healing and reclaiming lost values, and the powers of the Goddess' return to Western culture.

Another later interpretation of the descent myth, the story of Persephone and Demeter, celebrates the mother-daughter bond as well as the journey within. Demeter loses her daughter to the underworld but is finally reunited with her. It affirms the heritage passed on from mother to daughter and rejects the cultural pattern in which primary loyalties of mothers and daughters must be to men.

You will see the Demeter and Persephone archetypes in stories in this book that offer different views of the mother/daughter story.

The Cosmic Story

When I first began teaching college in 1988, I found few women willing to publicly express their anguish and confusion over their changing spiritual values. Now, in my current classes, spirituality has become a major component of the women's discussions and writings. Relegated to second place by patriarchy and taught to deny our instinctive connections with our inner power, we are searching for more meaningful connections as spiritual beings.

Some women perceive this as a return of the Goddess, implying a renewal of the feminine principle and an acceptance of equality and partnership between women and men. Her return means an acknowledgment of female power as a guiding force; it means the great and mysterious cycles of the universe; it means life energy at work. There are as many definitions as there are voices to express them.

The cosmic story of a culture, its cosmology, is the belief system that describes the nature of the universe. It includes creation myths and stories about the meaning of life that shed light on what lies beyond human perception. A cosmic story describes relationships between human beings and our relationships with living and non-living things of the earth.

An old cosmology that is re-emerging in the Western world reminds us of a matrilineal society in which the Goddess, or the Great Earth Mother, resided in honor, acknowledged as the creator of all that is. The myths surrounding her were lost or suppressed when patriarchal rule took over and replaced the Great Earth Mother with a male sky god. In the Mother-based belief system, all living and non-living things on the earth were valued and treated with respect. Some native traditions and indigenous cultures still live their lives within the framework of this ancient cosmology.

In Asia, stories of Buddhist women, both mythical and real, are used as examples and metaphors for life's journey. In these stories, middle-aged women who are not physical mothers may give birth to poems, songs, and books, or nurture other women, men, and children. They are viewed as incarnations of the Goddess in her creative, life-giving aspect.

The creation myths in this book reflect women's belief that as a culture we must reevaluate our relationship with the natural world and the feminine principle. We are in the midst of a time of question and change. We're reaffirming the value of the feminine and emerging triumphantly in wholeness. This is our collective quest.

Chapter 3: # Heal Your Past, Claim Your Future

How to Create Your Own Myth

There is a deep strength and power to be tapped by telling your story. I am continually impressed by it as I see women healing their psyches through personal mythmaking. I discovered this for myself from writing my own life as myth. When I started teaching college, I found that sharing it with my students encouraged other women to write their own myths. Later as my memories of childhood incest surfaced, I realized that I needed to rewrite the myth in order to reconcile two differing perceptions: my conscious memories of my childhood as a happy time with a perfect father and the recognition of a father who sexually abused me. It was difficult, but I was finally able to rewrite this myth. You will find the latest version of my myth, "So Good," as the last story in Part 2.

The women in my classes validate their life experiences when they tell their stories. They are often stunned that someone cares enough to listen without judgment. They are amazed at how much they begin to understand about themselves. They are creating new and meaningful myths that can change their lives.

Now I invite you to write your story, perhaps

for the first time in your life. This "life review" will give you new perspective and understanding about the journey that has taken you to where you stand today, and some insight into where you want to go from here.

I have used these exercises over and over again in my classes, and each time I am amazed at the richness and excitement of the experience. Women tell me:

> *"I can't believe that I've been through so much! It's amazing I've survived!"*

> *"It's the first time I've ever seen the patterns in my life. Now I can make changes."*

> *"My life is full of peaks and valleys."*

Exercise #1:
Travel through Time

Most people find this first exercise challenging and intriguing. It often takes several sessions, which is fine. Just be sure to come back after a break and, sooner or later, complete the exercise.

Get a notebook and pen, find a quiet place, turn on your answering machine, put the cat out, and sit comfortably, breathing deeply and calmly, as you let yourself go into a quiet inner space. Now travel back to your earliest memories and review your life from those memories to the present day. Start writing, letting things you remember come out without editing or judging. Record the significant events, the little things, the feelings, whatever occurs to you as you pass through the years.

If deep emotions and painful feelings arise, take a few deep breaths and remember that it is just a story—your interpretation of what has happened in your life up to this point. For many women, buried emotions surface, suggesting that there is some unfinished business to take care of. Pay attention to them when they come up, make a note of them, and continue with your story. You may have new insights into some event or interaction. Again, make note of them and move on.

When you are finished, take a few minutes to reflect on how it felt to write about yourself. What was it like for you? Did it flow easily? Did you find yourself getting stuck? What were your feelings?

Put the story aside for a day or two, then re-read it. What is your response now? You may want to add something you had forgotten or left out. You may find that some part is no longer essential. Don't edit your story at this point, but pay careful attention to the truth that you are telling about your life.

Exercise #2:
Division by Decades

The second step in the process of creating your personal myth will help you to see some patterns in your life experiences and your responses to change and transition.

Divide your life into decades. Write a synopsis of each decade. Look for themes. One woman described her life this way:

0-10. I lived for ten years in the same house with my parents and my sisters. A baby sister was born when I was five, and this changed my relationship with my mother particularly. I struggled to find my place in the family. School became an important outlet for me to define who I was.

10-20. I struggled through adolescence, trying to please my parents, but feeling lost and empty inside. I was afraid to be too smart at school, for fear boys would not like me. Sometimes I went along with the crowd just to be popular. Going to college was the most exciting time in my life.

20-30. I got pregnant my senior year and my parents were horrified. This was my most difficult time, struggling to keep the baby and survive as a single parent. I worked hard, and Mother reluctantly helped out with babysitting.

30-40. I feel I am alive again! I've remarried to an old boyfriend from college. I've found a job that I like. But I'm still struggling to find balance in my life. I'm tired most of the time.

Themes: Struggle, conformity, then rebellion. Re-connection with mother. New life, but continued struggle.

Another woman did this exercise in short notes:

0-10.   Born into alcoholic family.
        Moved eight times in ten years.
        Hard time making friends.

10-20. Became isolated personally and in community.
        Shame and anger toward father.
        Escaped through music and drama.

20-30. Went to community college, found mentor.
        Began singing locally.
        Drugs and alcohol abuse.
        Went into recovery.

Themes: Disconnection and isolation; anger, shame. Finding outlet. Overdoing. Recovery and creating new life.

When you're through writing, review your outline. Give it some time, for this will help you make sense of your life and find the patterns and themes that emerge. As you consider what you have written, ask yourself these questions:

1. *What are the major changes in my life?*

The changes may be external (moving, parents' divorce, loss of sibling, societal upheaval, loss of job), physical (illness or accident), or internal (realization that you are unhappy, challenged, afraid, triumphant).

2. *What patterns emerged?*

One woman was surprised to find out that she never stayed in a relationship for more than three years; she would soon move away to get out of it. She discovered that her life was filled with loss because her family moved every few years. Her depression was connected with buried anger toward her family for causing her to lose friendships and much-loved places.

3. *What were the marker events?*

Many women see their first menstrual period as an event that marks their emergence as women (sometimes with pride, more often with embarrassment or shame). Serious losses are generally important marker events. Divorce can be a marker that helps redefine who a woman is as a single person in a world of couples.

4.   What are the five most pivotal events from my story?

Identify the most salient events in your life and make sure they are included in your story. You may discover that what may have been pivotal a few years ago are no longer important, as you have new realizations or insights. My story, "So Good," was created as a result of this exercise. My five pivotal events were:

> Marriage
> Husband's alcoholism
> Divorce
> Incest memories
> Recovery

5.   Who are the main characters?

Major characters may be parents, siblings, friends, children, a spouse. They may emerge later as key figures in your myth.

Exercise #3:
Who Made the Choices?

Gather a few colored marking pens. Look over and reflect upon your major events and life changes. Color code the changes. Underline with one color those changes that were externally imposed. Use another color to indicate those changes that you consciously chose from the time you were a young adult until the present. Tally the results and ask yourself these questions:

1. *Are most of the changes in my life externally imposed?*

Many women are surprised to find that they have been passive for much of their adult life, subject to choices made by others. Whether for reasons of safety or for lack of will, they have gone along with the changes. Sometimes they feel angry with themselves or with the people who caused the change. If this is true for you, allow yourself to feel it, be with the anger. By acknowledging your feelings, they will have less power over you.

2. *Are most of my changes self-imposed?*

Some women are surprised to discover they were responsible for most of the changes. One woman realized that she moved from one job or relationship to another quickly, always looking for something new and exciting, and avoiding stability and quiet. She was addicted to excitement and chaos.

3. *Is there a balance of the two kinds of change?*

Some women see that their lives are a balance of externally and internally imposed changes. They feel empowered to determine the direction of their lives.

Exercise #4:
Core Values

As you review the changes of the past decade and look for the pattern, you'll see the values and beliefs that have guided you more recently. You may find changes here, as you go through the process of discovering new insights into yourself and how you relate to society's myths.

Think about your core values and principles. What is essential to your belief system, what values do you live your life by? These are the values you use to define yourself. Let symbols represent your core values, and draw four or five symbols on cards.

One woman found that a core value for her was creativity. The symbol that came to her was a light bulb nearly exploding. Realizing that creativity was one of the driving forces in her life, she revised her life to allow more time for creative projects.

As you reflect upon these core values and their symbols, consider what this means to you. What are you doing and what more can you do to express those values? If you fully expressed them, would it change your life in some way? How would you be seen by others?

Exercise #5:
Changing through Myth

Now it's time for "Once upon a time." Using a playful approach, you're going to invent a personal myth. You may write your story literally or as a fairy tale in which animals, plants, or inanimate objects represent characters in the story. Or you might prefer to write a poem, draw a picture, or compose a song. You could talk into a tape recorder or compose on a computer. Use the method that feels most comfortable to you, and plan to have some fun with it.

Settle yourself in a quiet spot and relax. Let go of any mental activity, thoughts, and worries. Let go of goals and outcomes. In other words, don't TRY! Just let this happen; there is no right or wrong, no result to strive for.

You might begin your story like this:

Once upon a time, there lived a poor man and woman who had five daughters and two sons. They lived in a magical land surrounded by the sea and had what they needed to be happy. In their garden grew a beautiful rose bush that had lived in its spot since the beginning of the magical land—long before the family grew around it.

One of my students, Cynthia Henry, personified her hero as a cat. Her story, the first myth in Part 2, begins:

In a time and a kingdom far away from now, a kitten was born. She was small, soft, and cuddly, and everyone loved to pet her furry coat. She was a good kitten, trained well to please all who came near. She was given a soft collar imprinted "Daughter."

An easy way to start your story is with the magical words "Once upon a time," and then let your myth unfold. Allow your spontaneity to take the story wherever it will go; editing and interpretation can come later. Try not to judge what comes. If an animal, plant, or object forms in your mind as you tell the story, let it happen.

The Greeks labeled the creative impulse our Muse. It's the intuitive self that is bursting to release creative energy through writing, poetry, dance, and music.

Balancing the Muse is our Editor, who edits, judges, and criticizes our creative effort. During this exercise, it's important to let your Muse have free rein. The Editor may be invited later to fine-tune your creation.

For now, sit quietly and let your myth lead you where it will. This is your chance to enjoy writing another version of your story.

When you're through, set your story aside for a time and then go back and read or listen to it. If a different name emerges as more appropriate for your hero, change her name. If you want to shift to a metaphorical hero, do so (animal, plant, etc.). Look for other metaphors. Women have used a myriad of rich metaphors to tell their stories: "emotionally wrapping my arms around it," "having fallen so far ... into a whirlpool of uncertainty," "bobsled going down a hill," "filling up my emptiness with food." One woman described midlife as a time when "I went into my house and cleaned out every corner ... and everything is upside down."

Look for an underlying theme. Give the myth a title. Ask yourself these questions:

How do I feel about my myth?

What new insights have I gained?

Are there surprises here?

How would I describe the hero?

Who is my enemy?

Did I really have choices? Why or why not?

What could I have done differently?

What do I *wish* I had done differently?

How might I change the ending?

Letting Go

Major life transitions can be painful. Even when we're eager for change, we feel a loss as we leave the old behind, whether it's an outworn idea, belief, or world view, or a literal thing or person. Before we can move into something new, we must be willing to undergo the pain of loss. Thus you may find that as you read your myth, you feel some sadness or regret. In my case, I was distraught that it had taken me so many years to learn certain lessons. "Why now?" I kept asking myself. "Why didn't I learn this long ago?"

The "If-only," "Why-didn't-I?" notions are unproductive at this point. Simply facing the reality of your life may enable you to move into a state of acceptance, and sometimes forgiveness, for yourself and for the other characters in your life story.

For many women, an almost magical moment, a turning point, occurs in the middle of the transition when they yield the victim role of previous years and accept responsibility for their lives from that moment on. I call this a moment of power, and it can be a transformative moment, for it indicates that the past has lost its hold. It is a moment of creativity and aliveness. This may happen to you as you write your personal myth and gain clarity on patterns and themes of your life. One woman's story revealed a pattern of moving every five years, which she suddenly saw was an avoidance of intimacy. If things got too close, she simply moved to another location and started over. When she realized this theme, she chose to create a new mythology in which she is the creator and protagonist of her life, no longer at the mercy of her inner psychological fears.

You may want to take some time to put closure on any unfinished business that your story has revealed. For many of the authors of these stories, writing their myths demanded that they let go of old resentments and anger and be willing to move on. Coming next in this section are some letting-go exercises to help you.

As you move through major life transitions and head in a new direction of your life, you may find your friendships changing. It can be painful to question old loyalties and shift allegiances, but by surrounding yourself with supportive friends and companions, you are much more likely to be successful in creating a new life story. By completing your unfinished business, you are reinventing yourself with a new storyline, plot, and cast of characters.

Often the women who wrote the myths have told me about revisions or new insights that came to them much later. I too have found that I am no longer a victim in my personal mythology. In fact, I am relieved to discover that I am weary of my life of high drama and am moving into a calmer state of mind and stronger recognition of the community of women.

Our stories change as our lives change. We

make new meanings of old experiences and integrate them into our life. That makes our stories richer, more interesting, and more relevant, because we find the patterns and themes change with shifting cultural myths. The movement never stops. We experience new wake-up calls, struggle to let go of the past, and discover that each time we move back into the world, we tell a new story with a stronger voice.

Letting-Go Exercises:

1. Look at your story and make a list of the people by whom you felt victimized. Write each of them a letter. Take time to express all your emotions regarding this issue. Put the letters aside for the time being. Later on, re-read each one and decide if you want to actually mail it. If not, burn it. You also may do this exercise by writing to people with whom you would like to make amends. The writing itself is a healing ritual.

2. Take a few minutes to sit quietly and think about where you have pain, either psychic or physical. Review your myth. What old part are you releasing? It may be a quality, a trait, or a limiting belief. Write it on a piece of paper and place it in a container. Release it, either through burning the paper or imagining it disappearing. Now, what new part of you, what quality, value, belief, or behavior, is waiting to be born? Affirm it.

3. Pretend there is a magic store in which you can buy any personal qualities you desire, such as generosity, sensitivity, tenderness, aggressiveness, power, and

so on. The price you pay is giving up some personal trait that you value. You are exchanging it for a value you desire even more.

Creating
New Rituals

A ritual is a myth transformed into action. By participating in rituals, your myths become real. Many women are finding that rituals and celebrations, often over-looked in our busy lives, help us deal with the loss of "what was" and of the unknown that lies ahead.

Looking back on my life, I realize I have always been searching for meaningful ritual—birthday parties, outings in nature, ceremonial gatherings as a Camp Fire girl, rituals in sororities, and celebrations of community through church and women's groups.

Ancient cultures had rites of passage that gave stability and strength to the participants. These rituals pro-vided a bridge between the inner and outer worlds, in-creasing one's balance, strength, energy, and comfort. Today women are creating new rituals and ceremonies to mark rites of passage: menarche for their daughters, meno-pause, career changes, birthdays, death of a parent. All rituals center around transition—changes that have hap-pened, are happening, or may happen. Transitions are be-ginnings, mergings, cycles, and endings.

Mark the important events in your life that are revealed in your myth, particularly any recent beginning or ending. Examples are births, new homes, corporate merger, new housemate, divorce, and retirement. Other rituals honor notable events, such as menarche, menopause, and anniversaries.

Whenever you feel an imbalance in your life, ritual can help. One woman, after reviewing her life story, created a powerful letting-go ritual. She methodically went through her personal belongings, journals and all, clearing out what was the "old" self. Gathering it up into a huge bundle, she placed it on a sheet that she had painted with archetypal symbols and burned it in a bonfire at the beach.

Designing a Ritual

To help you design your own ritual, here are a few guidelines.

1. Preparation. Decide what you want to accomplish. Why are you doing it? What mood do you want to create? Who would you like to be present?

2. Planning. The most important aspect of this phase is to decide what you want to recognize, honor, or heal. Ask yourself this question, "What quality do I want to bring into our hearts?" This will help you choose the time and setting for your ritual.

3. Symbols. Choose a few objects that have special meaning to you. Decide how you'd like to use song, storytelling, drumming, or poetry. Flowers, background music, candles, food, and natural objects all contribute to a sense of beauty. Pay attention to any colors, symbols, and metaphors that emerged in your myth.

As I approached my sixtieth birthday, I felt a

strong desire to gather together all of the significant women in my life, to celebrate community and to show my appreciation for their support in my life journey. In that magical circle were thirty females of all ages, including my two-year-old granddaughter and three women in their seventies. All of the women had shared my sorrows and joys. That three-hour celebration honored my passage into the place of the crone, or wise woman.

Planning my birthday party was an emotional experience. My initial intention was to create a ritual that let my friends know my appreciation for their parts as characters in my life story. However, as I moved deeper into the planning, I realized that I also wanted something from them. It was difficult to ask, but I invited each of the women to share something special about our relationship.

If you are designing a celebration for yourself, watch out for the old voice that asks, "Do I really deserve this?"

Conducting a Ritual

Here are a few suggestions for conducting your ritual.

1. Create a sacred space. The Greeks called this *temenos*, indicating a place of wholeness and unity. Start by greeting people, introducing them, and sharing the intention. You may want to invoke the direction of larger energies, the Goddess, the spirits of your ancestors, or whatever is meaningful to you. Light a candle or use a moment of silence, prayers, or group meditation to invoke your sacred space.

2. Choose an activity. All rituals consist of some action in which you choose to transform the desired changes from the inner to the outer world. You might plant a seed or a tree, burn a photo, connect the group with a ribbon, create drawings, clay sculpture, or group collage, share poems and stories, make masks, or play musical instruments.

3. Create a closing. Close with some act of completion, such as a blessing, a song, a poem, or silence. It is essential to leave space for the transition between the ceremony and the next activity, whether it be sharing food or the guests leaving.

4. Reflect. What was it that you received? What really happened in that gathering of people?

Beck and Metrick, in *The Art of Ritual*, state, "Although the sacred quality of the ritual may lead you to believe that what has occurred in that time belongs only to that time, the truth is that the rareness of the occasion may have left you with special and valuable gifts." The most important gifts I received at my party were the love of my women friends and family members, and the power of community.

As you create your own rituals to symbolize, share, or put closure on events in your personal myth, you join with others to embark on the writing of a new mythology.

Claim
Your Future

We are done with the past and are beginning to envision a different future. An exciting concept that I have shared with many of my classes is the idea of Future Pull, presented in Land and Jarman's book, *Breakpoint and Beyond*. Instead of being pushed by the past—events, experiences, people, beliefs—we can envision the perfect future we desire, commit to it, and let that energy pull us toward the vision. It is a dramatic paradigm shift, and one that assists us in truly reinventing ourselves according to new beliefs, values, and an empowered sense of ourselves as women. This reinvention often means reclaiming parts of ourselves that have been lost as we grew up.

Exercise #1:
Imagine a Miracle

To get a glimpse of your future, sit quietly for a few minutes. Imagine yourself five years from now and ask, "If there were a miracle right now, what would my life look like?"

1. What images or symbols emerge?
2. Who is included in your vision?
3. What would be your first step today in achieving that vision?
4. Create an affirmation that supports the vision, using the present tense, such as: "I am creating a healing environment for my family," or "I am healthy and strong."

Exercise #2:
Find Your Purpose

Your purpose inspires and gives meaning to your life. Most of us want to make a difference in the world. The best way to do that is to discover our unique talents and abilities and find ways to express them. By following the path that has heart and meaning for us, we connect with others of similar passion. Ask yourself these questions:

1. What do I love to do?
2. What makes me happy?
3. What do I dream of doing or becoming?
4. How can I express my creativity? My spirituality?

One woman realized as she did this exercise that she felt more alive in her off-work hours than at work in a social services office. Reevaluating her life at age 50, she started a new business in which she did "housecare." Tapping into her previously suppressed creative ability, she worked with clients to bring aliveness and joy into their homes.

Exercise #3:
Map the Future

This exercise shows how you set your priorities and use your time. It reveals what is missing in your life. Then you begin to let the future pull you forward intentionally.

1. Imagine your typical week. Think about all the activities and functions you perform, the roles you play, the responsibilities you have, the things you like to do. See yourself in all of these aspects of your life, being aware

of how much time and importance you give to each one.

Now make a map of your life on a large circle. Divide the shape into sections that represent those aspects you have visualized. Let each section proportionally represent the amount of time that you give to each aspect. Identify every section with a symbol, color, image, word, or phrase. Study your map and ask yourself these questions: Are there any aspects of my life that I'd like to change? Are there some I'd like to limit or drop? Are some good things missing?

2. Make a new map of a week as you would like it to be, including all the things you'd like to be doing and experiencing. Again, let each section reflect how important it really is to you.

3. Look at the changes you put into your new map. Plan how you will actually implement these changes in the coming month. Keep track of your progress and check back in a week or so to see how you are doing.

Exercise #4:
Commit to Your Vision

It seems to be a law of nature that resistance follows intention. Once you move toward a goal, you may be discouraged to find obstacles in your way. You will be more successful in achieving your vision if you consider these questions.

1. How strong is my intention? How much do I really want it to happen?
2. What will I have to give up?

3. What am I resisting?
4. Where can I find support as I move toward my goal?

One woman was at a major crossroads. Having struggled for years over whether to get pregnant or not, she realized from this exercise that her vision did not include a baby. She compensated for the loss of her image of motherhood with a new exciting creative undertaking: photography. Her vision of herself as a nature photographer was affirmed when a nature journal printed one of her photographs in its fall edition.

As the composer and conductor of your life, you take steps down a new, sometimes unfamiliar path, emboldened by your newly found wisdom, heartened by your courage, and excited by your new vision of the future. You begin to share your story with others, inspiring them to take risks. Thus you become part of the new collective mythology offered as a legacy to future generations of women.

Remember to continually ask yourself these questions: "Where am I going, and who's going with me?" You might be surprised by the answers. You may find yourself writing a new or different myth, or continuing the one you've written. Happily ever after is just the beginning.

PART 2: WOMEN'S NEW MYTHS

ow for the myths. They were created by women of all ages who returned to school during a time of major transition. For some women, the transitions were personal: divorce, relationship change, physical health. For others, the change was professional: reentry from full-time homemaking, job dissatisfaction, career change, or burnout. Many of the women were experiencing crises in their spiritual lives. All of them intentionally chose a college setting as their path of self-discovery.

Behind each story is a theme of our culture, with its messages, dictates, and stereotypical male/female roles. Uncovering these themes is a powerful tool you can use to heal yourself, redirect your life, and reclaim your future.

Read the stories slowly. After you read each one, wait quietly and let the meanings emerge. You may be reminded of favorite childhood myths or fairy tales. The myths may contain archetypes, symbols, and metaphors that are familiar. You might want to make notes of connections, insights, questions, and emotional responses to the story. These are personal myths, but each has a collective meaning as well that may resonate with your own experience.

You will find many of the goddess archetypes discussed earlier. Look especially for ways in which the women discard old roles or archetypes and begin expressing new ones. Some myths have an environmental theme and encourage us to live in harmony with the natural world. Notice that many of the myths tell stories of redemption: journeying into dark places where the hero retrieves some lost part of herself. Despite obstacles, resistance, and fear, the hero ultimately finds resolution of the problem, and perhaps peace and happiness.

It is a journey toward wholeness.

The Lost Purr

Cynthia L. Henry

In a time and a kingdom far away from now, a kitten was born. She was small, soft, and cuddly, and everyone loved to pet her furry coat. She was a good kitten, trained well to please all who came near. She was given a soft collar imprinted "Daughter."

Now it came to pass that when this kitten became a full-grown cat, she was given to a Prince to grace his home and to please him. She was given a new collar and the name of "Wife." Into her new home Cat brought a simple tapestry bag that was to be used to hold memories and treasures. Because Cat believed this was true happiness, her Purr rang loud and filled the home.

Cat was blessed with three fine kittens, each special and unique in its own way. Now her collar read "Wife" and "Mother," and Cat added three precious jewels to the collar and they shone brightly as each kitten grew. In her tapestry bag, Cat placed memories she treasured, and as she added more and more, the bag itself appeared to take on an inward radiance. Many priceless treasures were added to the bag through the years: some sad, some full of pride, some content, but always with love.

As the years passed, while she tried to please

the Prince, Cat began to feel his discontentment. She sensed an overwhelming power that did not come from her, but from the Prince, and it beat down on her head and heart with sadness. The Prince was unhappy—unhappy with Cat, with the kittens, and with his life in the kingdom.

The memories she placed in the tapestry bag grew dull and gray as Cat tried harder and harder to please the Prince. One day Cat noticed that her Purr no longer echoed in the halls of the castle. The kittens searched with Cat throughout the kingdom, but the Purr was gone.

The Prince began to make comments like:

"You are not pretty enough. You disgrace me in front of the other Princes."

"This castle is not pleasing to me. Work harder to bring it to my level."

"You are not smart enough to sit with other Princes' cats."

"Your kittens displease me."

"I want to be a Prince who represents lavishness, power, and youth. You are too reserved, too quiet to be with my friends."

His remarks came in black rolling clouds, and Cat believed them because she was well trained to try to please without question. "After all," she thought, "he is my master. I must not be good enough, because he is smarter and better educated than me. I'm just a plain little Cat with three precious kittens."

So Cat worked harder to become the image the Prince wanted her to be. But the Purr remained lost and Cat grew tired. She no longer knew how to be happy or even to know what collar to wear in the castle, which now was dark with the Prince's discontent. Tears were damaging the tapestry bag, the kittens grew sad, and Cat no longer knew who she was or was supposed to be.

By now the tapestry bag was a dull shade and tattered and torn. But the inside still glowed, holding the jewels of memories and hopes.

One day the Prince came into Cat's chambers and announced, "You have displeased me. I have status amongst my friends and in the community. You, Cat, are unworthy of this Prince and his power. Therefore, you will be on your own to survive and to raise your kittens." And with these cruel words, he left.

The Cat was very, very sad, and she wept, staining her tapestry bag still more. But she was a strong cat, ready to accept the challenges that life gave her. She removed her collar and took her kittens with her to find the path back to happiness. The kittens pulled in close to their mother, and even when the days were rough, Cat kept going on her quest to find who she was.

She searched and worked, and after a time the day came when she decided she needed a new collar, one that showed who she really was. So she melted down her "Daughter," "Wife," and "Mother" collars and pre-served the essence of each. She formed, polished, and etched, and she created the softest, most golden collar of all. She placed it around her neck, viewed it in a mirror, and was pleased. This was by far the loveliest collar. It glowed with light, and the three jewels sparkled. Cat's name was etched deeply into the gold. It proclaimed to the world, "I Am Who I Am." And Cat was content with the name.

At the same time, somehow, magically, the tapestry bag also took on a new glow. The colors brightened and the bag seemed to become new again. And one day, while she was adding memories, Cat heard a rumbling deep inside the bag. She drew her kittens near and opened the bag wide. The rumbling grew louder, and the family drew back in fear.

Suddenly, from deep within, the rumbling burst into the air. And now the Cat smiled. The rumbling was her lost Purr, and as it rolled around, it caressed Cat and her kittens with joy and peace. The Purr was found. And the cat, her kittens, and her grand-kittens lived happily for the rest of their time.

A Tale of Becoming

Teresa R. Diaz

nce upon a time in a place far, far away, there was a small shining star who wished for a life on Earth. She went to the One Who Decides and asked, "When shall it be my time?"

"Not yet, small bright one, not yet," answered the One Who Decides. Time passed very slowly for the small bright one. Again, she came before the One Who Decides and asked, "When shall it be my time?" She was growing impatient.

"Practice patience, small bright one," answered the One Who Decides. The small bright one really did try her best to be patient, but it was taking so long! Earth, so far away and so beautiful, looked like a wonderful place to her. She yearned to go.

One evening, after a full day of practicing patience, and once again being told her time had not yet come, she decided she had waited long enough. She collected all her brightness into a small, glimmering ball and with a mighty effort flung herself all the way to Earth.

For a time, it seemed as if her ball of brightness would not be enough to get her there. But she was determined and kept going. She came closer and closer, and at last she was on Earth where she could relax and simply float to the surface. But oh, she was so very tired. Her small bright light had become dim, and she needed a soft, warm place to rest. It took a long while, but eventually her small bright light found a home and grew bright again. In fact, she was brighter than ever before! She had a mother and father to love and care for her. And so her time on Earth began.

Meanwhile, the One Who Decides had been carefully watching the small bright one. She was not surprised. The small bright one would learn her lessons with much difficulty. The pain would be great, but she had made her choice. The One Who Decides lovingly divided herself so she could continue to watch over the small bright one during her growing time on Earth. She would need many blessings of light and guidance.

Life went along for the small bright one. Sometimes, tiny nudges in her being told her that something was not quite right, but she would quickly shake them off and run outside to play so she wouldn't have to think about them.

When she was two years old, the first crack appeared. It was a summer day, and her family was on a walk in the forest. A giant log had been placed across a creek as a bridge. The father would allow no one to help the small bright one across. He didn't understand her terror of falling into the water and losing her light forever. The mother wanted to reach out to help her, but the father was much stronger than the mother.

The small bright one stood helpless and frightened. The father dragged the mother away down the trail and around the bend. They were gone! She was left alone. With a sobbing breath, the small bright one gathered all her brightness into a small, small ball and began to slowly cross the log. The One Who Decides watched with concern and sadness. In the middle of the log, the small bright one could no longer hold onto her bright ball. Her brightness flew apart.

At that moment, she realized what she had done when she refused to follow the way of the One Who Decides. She had chosen a mother and a father who did not know how to care for her in ways that would allow her to flourish. She raised her arms in anguished plea to the heavens and knew then that the choice was final. She had chosen to come to Earth in her own way, and now she must follow that path. So the small one hid her bright part and began to care for herself. The One Who Decides breathed a heavy sigh. Thus began a long, dark time of lostness.

On the path the small one had chosen, many shadows and snarling dragons appeared, seeking to steal her light. They grabbed for it, chased her, tried to force her to give it up. But she had hidden it well, deep in a cave, and placed her own ferocious and attentive dragon at the entrance. Through this time of darkness the One Who Decides watched and waited. The small one left her home and her mother and father and began her quest in the world. The shadows followed. She was surrounded by shadows.

One day, quite unexpectedly, in the dark, the small one bumped into something very large. Huge, in fact. She had no idea what it was. The dragon who guarded the cave where the brightness was hidden roared mightily. The huge something didn't budge. So the small one buried the bright part even deeper and then began to consider what had bumped her. What was that huge something?

A memory washed over her; she remembered that a long time ago tiny nudges in her being had bothered her. Now, all of a sudden, they weren't tiny anymore. They had grown huge and were bumping her. The waves of remembering overwhelmed her.

The dragon at the entrance was roaring ceaselessly now. The small one could barely keep from flying apart. The One Who Decides was watching and knew the time had come to gently release the vacuum the small bright one had placed around herself. The rest was up to her.

Slowly she became aware of who she was and began to remember. She found ways to honor the precious bright part she had buried deep in the cave. She convinced the dragon to go get a new job elsewhere, and she let the small bright part of herself out of the dark place and made friends with her. She learned how to care for her, nourish her, and play with her. It was time to invite her back, to bring the small bright part into herself. The One Who Decides breathed a sigh of relief and sparkled with joy. The small bright one was ready to share her small bright part.

As things work out, a large star came by and chose to learn how to care for and honor her small bright part. As loving attention to a garden results in a bountiful harvest, so it was for the small bright one. With love and care, she thrived and eventually grew into a grand star with many sparkles around her. Her brightness guided many through the shadows. The One Who Decides and the One Who Emerged became One. And the journey continues ...

The Fisherwoman and Her Daughter

Abigail Lambert

Once there was a fisherwoman who lived in a dwelling at the edge of a large lake. It was a beautiful lake, but the fisherwoman knew that at one end a dangerous giant eel lived in a huge cave. She was careful to stay away from that part of the lake.

Early each morning, the fisherwoman would gather up her nets and weights and basket and stroll along the sand by the lake until she came to just the right spot to begin her work. There she would cast her nets, sit on a fallen tree trunk, and watch the sun rise over the trees. Sometimes the big turtle who lived in the lake came by. He was old and wise, and he and the fisherwoman would talk quietly as they basked in the sun.

By lunchtime the nets would be full of silvery, squirming fish. The fisherwoman then pulled in the nets and poured the fish into her basket before she began the leisurely walk back to her hut. She always left a few scraps for her friend, the turtle.

One day the fisherwoman wakened with a terrible pain and could not rise from her bed. She lay under the covers moaning, and soon a small bird flew to a branch outside her window and asked, "Why are you not out fishing as usual?"

The fisherwoman groaned. "I am ill," she said. "I am in pain."

Upon hearing this, the bird began to sing. The woman was surprised and a little upset.

"Little bird, why do you sound so happy when I feel so bad?" she asked.

The bird replied, "You foolish woman, I am happy because you are going to have a baby girl today. And she will bring you much happiness."

The bird was right. The fisherwoman soon gave birth to a healthy baby girl. She named her Llenelen, which means "joy," because the bird told her that the child would bring happiness. Indeed, the fisherwoman's life became brighter than it had ever been before. After each morning's work, she would carry her basket of fish on one arm and the baby Llenelen on the other arm back to the hut. The mother and daughter would sit for hours in the sun playing with shells and pebbles, watching the water birds, and taking a nap now and then. As Llenelen grew, she and her mother worked and played together and were as happy as two people can be. They loved to dance by the shore of the lake. The fisherwoman adored her precious daughter, and only occasionally glanced nervously across the lake toward the ominous cave of the giant eel.

In spite of her contentment, Llenelen began to wonder about the world that lay beyond the lake. When she mentioned this, her mother became angry. Sometimes her mother seemed angry for no reason. Then Llenelen was afraid that her mother might cease to love her, and she tried extra hard to please her.

One day, while the two were out fishing, they heard a terrible noise. They looked up and were horrified to see an enormous scaly head rise out of the water. A creature with monstrous fangs and rolling green eyes rose up from the lake, grabbed Llenelen in its hideous mouth, and dragged her down beneath the waves.

The mother screamed in anguish and fell upon the sand. She wept in grief for three days and three nights, and on the morning of the fourth day she looked up into the blue and gold sky and wondered aloud, "Why am I weeping? I can no longer remember. I only know I have suffered a loss and am too weak to go on living." She lay back and prepared to die.

The little bird hopped to her again and sat on her chest and looked at her with his beady black eyes. He asked, "Why are you waiting for death? It is not your time to die."

The fisherwoman answered, "I am too weak to live, for I have lost something precious."

"What did you lose?"

She thought for awhile. "I think I have lost a part of myself," she said.

"You silly woman, your tears have erased your memory. Your daughter was swallowed by the giant eel that lives in the lake. That is what you have lost."

The fisherwoman moaned as she remembered. "Then all is indeed lost and I might as well die."

The insistent bird started to peck the woman's

skin. Wearily she swatted him from her chest. He hopped to her shoulder and began to sing in her ear. She sat up and asked, "What possible reason could you have for singing at a time like this?"

"Because now we must go and search for your daughter," the bird chirped.

As the giant eel carried her down under the water, Llenelen became so frightened she lapsed into unconsciousness. When she awoke, she looked around in wonder. She was alone in a huge underwater cave that was piled high with mountains of gold coins and jewels. Scattered over the cave floor were many bones.

The giant eel slithered into the cave and said in a cold, watery voice, "This is where I keep all of my treasures. When I am finished with you, your bones shall lie with the others."

"Please don't eat me, Great Eel," Llenelen begged. "I will do whatever you wish, but please spare me."

The giant eel chuckled. "Can you dance, little human? If you can dance well, one of my sons may be persuaded to make you his wife."

And so it came to pass that Llenelen found herself dancing, not happily by the lake shore, but in misery for the giant eel's many sons. The sons were rude and loud, and they insisted that she dance naked for them, night after night for so many nights Llenelen lost count of them. She was ashamed of her nakedness, and after awhile she wondered if she would ever have the courage to lift her head up again.

The fisherwoman built a raft. She hoped to float out on the lake and search for her lost daughter. But each time she was almost ready to sail, she noticed some chore that needed her attention and she put off her search, telling herself she would get to it the next day. After weeks of this, the bird flew in and perched on her head. "Why aren't you out searching for your daughter?" he asked.

"Go away and leave me alone. I'm busy," said the mother, shaking her head vigorously to dislodge the bird.

The bird flew to the windowsill. "I can see you are busy. But your most important task has yet to be done. What's keeping you from getting started?"

The fisherwoman hung her head. She thought for awhile and then, with lowered eyes, told the bird what she had been too ashamed to admit even to herself. "I love my daughter," she whispered. "I miss her deeply. But I'm frightened of the giant eel."

"Don't be too hard on yourself," the bird advised. "Anybody in their right mind would be afraid of that monster. If it will make it easier for you, I'll fly above you over the lake and warn you when the eel begins to surface."

So the mother climbed onto the raft, pushed off with a long stick, and floated over the water, looking for Llenelen. She peered down into the murky depths and called her daughter many times, but never saw any sign of her or the eel.

In the giant eel's cave, Llenelen was desperate to escape. She schemed and planned, but every time she tried to get away, the eel found out and blocked her way. After her last attempt, as she lay discouraged on her mat of dried grass, she heard a soft noise and, looking up, saw a large black and green turtle squatting by the doorway. "I am a friend, Llenelen," said the turtle. "I have come from the surface of the lake. Your mother is very worried, and she is searching for you as we speak."

Sadly Llenelen said, "I have tried to escape, turtle, but it never works. And now the thought of returning to my mother fills me with shame."

"Do not fear your mother's anger or judgment for what has befallen you, Llenelen. She too is ashamed. All the while you were growing up, she knew about the giant eel here at the bottom of the lake. She was afraid that some day you would be pulled down just as she was many years ago, but she did not know how to prevent it. This has been the source of her great inner anger."

The turtle crawled closer to Llenelen and spoke again. "You must come with me and return to the surface of the lake. Escape now, or your mother may never be able to find you."

And so Llenelen climbed on the turtle's back, and together they swam out of the cave. The giant eel and his terrible sons were nowhere to be seen.

When they reached the surface, the sunlight dazzled her eyes. But as her vision cleared, Llenelen could see her mother across the lake, floating on the raft, gazing into the water and calling her name.

"Mother!" she cried.

With a shout of joy, the fisherwoman paddled toward her daughter, who jumped from the turtle's back and began swimming to meet her. They met in the middle of the lake, and Llenelen climbed aboard the raft and into her mother's waiting arms.

For days they floated, arm-in-arm upon the smooth shining water, while the little bird and the old turtle kept watch for any sign of danger from below.

The Colors

Barbara Sawyer

sn't she darling!" everyone said.
"Is she real?" someone asked.

In the kingdom of Properville, the princess was VERY polite. She did all the things a proper young princess should do. She learned to curtsy, to say

"Thank you!"

and

"Please?"

She never cried, except when she was alone in her room at the top of the palace tower.

She was a good little princess. She never forgot that Daddy and Mommy were the King and Queen, that they must always be treated in a special way. When she felt lonely or unhappy she would remind herself that she was, after all, a very lucky princess with nothing to be unhappy about. She should be grateful that things were so-o-o-o good ...

even

if

they

didn't

always

feel

that

way!

The princess had a gift. She had a color of her very own. The color was given to her by the Magic Person just before she was born. The Magic Person left gifts for all the boys and girls born in the Kingdom of Properville, and each one was different. But the Magic Person never left instructions or told the children what they were to do with their gifts. The Magic Person did not explain how the gifts worked or how to take care of them. When the princess was old enough to think about it, she thought this was strange. Everything else in her life seemed to be explained, and the grown-up people were always telling her

HOW to do things

HOW to take care of things

HOW to act

HOW to feel

and WHAT to do.

So she never really understood the Magic Person or the gift.

When the princess was small, she wore her color often. When her friends came to the palace to play, they would wear their colors too. They danced and laughed, and soon the nursery would become very bright. All their colors, scrambled together, wiggled and sparkled. Sometimes you could hear music. Once in awhile the children would invite the Magic Person to dance with them, but that was only make-believe, because the grown-ups said the Magic Person didn't exist. The grown-ups didn't wear colors.

Gradually, as they grew older, the princess and her friends wore their colors less often. When her friends came to play, they wanted games and trinkets to play with. Little by little the nursery came to look like every other room in the palace, full of things that were

appropriately designed,

neatly arranged,

well coordinated,

and VERY practical!

One day the princess realized that it was time to put her color away. She wasn't sure why,

but she knew

she should put it away.

Colors were one of the things no one talked about, and, being such a good little princess, she didn't ask embarrassing questions. She climbed the attic stairs and found a box and lined it with white tissue paper. She carefully placed her color in the box, closed the lid so that none of the color could escape, and tied the box with a ribbon. When she had finished, she slipped the box under her bed.

The princess had done this sort of thing before. Under her bed you could find all kinds of things that she had put away. There was a box for her ballerina dreams, a box full of reindeer, and one with a stuffed St. Nicholas. There was one for her best bride doll, and one full of make-believe friends she had outgrown. There was a baseball glove, and a microscope, and a blue ribbon for being the fastest runner in the fourth grade.

The little princess grew to be a fine young woman. Everyone in the Kingdom of Properville respected and loved her. She was all that a good princess should be.

Then a visitor came to the palace. He was a strange old man, with a long white beard. His smile was gentle and his eyes had a wise and faraway look. AND he wore colors!

The princess had not seen colors for so many years that at first she wasn't sure what they were, or if they were real. For a brief moment she remembered something about a Magic Person, but the memory was foggy and not at all sensible, and it quickly faded away.

The old man and the princess became fast friends. They shared poetry, music, and secrets together. In time, they came to know one another by their real names.

One day, following a storm, the old man and the princess went for a walk in the rose garden. The sun was just peeking through the clouds as the old man pointed to the rainbow in the sky and began to tell the princess a story.

"Once upon a time," he said, "all the colors of the rainbow belonged to the people. But colors need to be cared for. If they are ignored or discounted, they wander away and they hide in the rainbow. Most of the time the colors are too shy to show themselves, but once in a while, like today, they dare to visit the kingdom and the people to whom they once belonged.

"It only happens when the rains have washed away the darkness and the sun brings promise," the old man continued. "People always 'oo' and 'ah' over the beauty of the rainbow, but they never recognize the colors that belong to them. The colors wait patiently, hoping, but eventually they drift off again, a little sadder than before."

With those words, the princess remembered the box. "Excuse me," she said politely and ran, two steps at a time, to her room in the tower. She knelt and pulled the box from under the bed. It was covered with dust. The princess trembled as she held it for the first time in many years. She blew the dust away, untied the ribbon, and sat looking at the box. She was afraid to open it.

Slowly she lifted the lid, and the color crept out. It was mellow. It was gentle. It was warm. As the princess watched the color, she remembered how much she had loved it. She noticed that her color was no longer just one color. Flecks of other colors seemed to mingle and stretch within it. Her color began to drift about the room, exploring freedom and movement after being in the box for so long.

The princess stood and wrapped the color around her shoulders. She was surprised at how well it fit, and how rich and fine it was. At first she felt like crying, the way she had felt long ago when she was lost in the department store. Then she recalled how it felt to be found, and she wanted to laugh and dance. As she danced, wrapped in color, a fog lifted and with joy she remembered the colors in the nursery. She sat on the floor and hugged her color, feeling warm and safe, like coming home.

The princess went to find the old man in the garden. She wanted to thank him for the rainbow story and for helping her to remember. The sun shone brightly, and drops of water sparkled on the leaves and petals of rosebuds. Spiders climbed their stalks, butterflies stretched their wings. But the old man was gone.

As the princess turned to go, the gardener's child ran up and handed her a note. She unfolded it, and this is what she read:

It's time!

BE THE MAGIC PERSON.

Cicada Junction

Jody I. Robindottir

nce upon a time in the luxuriant Amazon rain forest, there lived a huge family of cicadas. They were blessed with brilliant coloring and had glossy spring-green wings that gleamed in the sun. All the cicadas had tymbals on their abdomens that allowed them to make a rich calling noise. They used this gift as a means of communication and a way of expressing their joy of life.

One night, the male cicadas, like the males of most species, were down at the bar bragging of their conquests and dreaming of more. A large group decided that they would go adventuring to the north. There would be more room and more food and a better variety, or so they claimed. And off they went to convince the female cicadas to accompany them. The females, however, said they didn't want to leave their lush green tropical forest.

So the males went to the Goddess. When the Goddess learned that they were dissatisfied with the beautiful Garden she had given them, She was quite offended. She rebuffed them and refused to help them secure the females' compliance or bless their journey.

"Who cares?" snorted Hugo, the head honcho of the cicadas. "We'll find us a male god or make one up."

That appalled even some of the most belligerent male cicadas, so a large number defected from the group that had decided to migrate north. Hugo, surprised at this insubordination and feeling threatened at having less than total power, had to come up with a plan. He devised a new call on his tymbal. He boasted that this was a special message from the male god he had discovered. The god wanted them to go north, Hugo said. In fact, this new deity demanded it, and his power was almighty and if they didn't listen to him they were bound for terrible destruction, Hugo said.

The Goddess, witnessing all this with her hands on her hips, said "Hmmm." She knew what awaited them in the north. She felt compassion for her misguided cicadas, so she went to the females and tried to dissuade them from embarking with the males. Some of the females heeded her warnings, but some were so enamored with their mates or so fearful of Hugo's threats that they agreed to take up with the new male god. They beat their tymbals in his praise.

Now a great flurry of activity began as the cicadas prepared for their journey. Tymbals seemed to be constantly throbbing and beating. And then, whoosh! They were off, headed northward, with Hugo proudly in the lead. After a long and tedious journey, they touched down in the new country. There they found that the leaves were changing color, something that never happened in their native habitat.

"Aark, these leaves are colorful but they are dry. No juice. We can't eat them. Let's ask the great and omnipotent god what we should do," they said. The god, according to Hugo, said that they had all sinned and come short of the glory and deserved to die on dry leaves.

The Goddess was watching this, tapping her foot all the while. She knew they were in for even greater difficulties—namely snow. She tapped and tapped and waited for them to come to her. The females, sensing deep trouble, gathered together and decided to try to approach the Goddess. Maybe she would help them, even though they had deserted her. "What shall we do, Great Mother?"

"You foolish cicadas did as I told you not to do. Now there is a price to be paid. I will go into council and see if I can relieve your problems."

"Thank you, Goddess, but please hurry," they said in unison.

"I will meet you in the grove of sycamores over by the rushing stream in a short while," said the Goddess. "Bring your mates and all the rest of the cicadas."

The small group of female cicadas went quickly to get their mates and the other cicadas so they could resolve their terrible plight.

The anxious beating of tymbals greeted the Goddess as she stepped down from her heavenly flowery ladder. "My precious cicadas, you do not realize the enormous threat that imperils you. This country will become very cold in a few moons. You have no idea how cold. You were not designed to withstand icy winds and snow. There will be nothing for you to eat.

"You made your choice and I cannot undo it. Nevertheless, in my compassion I have come up with a plan that will allow your species to survive. You will go underground for thirteen or seventeen years, depending on the amount of sunlight in the areas you now inhabit. There you will manage to live by eating the roots of trees. You will come above ground when the sun shines brightest in this region. In order to reproduce, the females will have to give up their tymbals. Every thirteen to seventeen years you will come to the surface to mate."

"Oh my, oh my," cried one small female cicada, as her green wings shimmered in the morning sun. "My granddaughters will no longer be able to have a tymbal and all of us will have to live underground for thirteen or maybe even seventeen years. It is almost unbearable. Our beautiful green wings will become almost useless."

"And to think that we didn't even want to come," mourned another female cicada.

After a few weeks, white stuff began to fall from the clouds. It was soft and beautiful, but all the cicadas were shivering. They called upon the Goddess once again.

"Why have you not gone underground as I instructed?" she inquired of the gathered cicadas.

"How do we do that? We have only weak forelegs," several cicadas replied.

The Goddess sighed. "I shall indulge you once again. I will give you great strength in your forelegs to dig with. And now you must hurry, for an early winter approaches. Go!" cried the Goddess, and she vanished up her rosebud-entwined ladder in a flurry of stars and snowflakes.

Immediately the cicadas felt their forelegs grow stronger. They were powerful enough to dig into the earth, and dig they did, for the air was growing colder by the minute.

As they dug, they sang a sad song about the beautiful home they had left behind. "This is the lesson of the cicada," they sang. "Know your true home, and never forget to honor the Goddess."

The Mirage Mirror

Mary Jane Gavette

nce upon a time, an opossum, an eagle, a chameleon, a mouse, a ferret, a weasel, and a fox lived together on a farm. The farm lay in a beautiful valley with a river running through it. It was a wondrous place of trees and fields and radiant wild flowers. The river flowed past the farm with constancy and bestowed life-giving moisture to the seven friends and the other animals on the farm, and the trees and fields provided homes and food and a place to play.

The opossum, the chameleon, the mouse, the ferret, the weasel, the eagle, and the fox loved it on the farm. They thought the world outside it was dangerous and frightful, and they protected themselves from it by never leaving the farm. But as time passed, the outside world began encroaching upon their little kingdom, and so the animals learned different ways of being in order to protect themselves. The opossum learned to play dead, the chameleon learned to change color, the mouse learned to hide, the ferret learned to hunt, the weasel learned to deceive, the eagle learned to use its wings, and the fox learned to be clever.

The seven friends were seldom apart. They played together, ate together, worked together, and squabbled among themselves just as all good friends sometimes do. They were possessive of each other and very frightened that one of them would get hurt.

When Eagle ventured out alone to try her wings, Mouse was so afraid for her that she hid in the grass, and Opossum plopped right down where she was and played dead. Weasel and Ferret scolded Eagle and warned her not to leave the group. Chameleon was so frightened she changed colors over and over again trying to make Eagle change her mind, and Fox cleverly sabotaged Eagle's attempt. Eagle listened to her friends and became afraid, too. She stayed at home in the safety of the group.

On another occasion, Ferret decided to take a risk and explore life outside the kingdom. The other six friends panicked at the thought of Ferret leaving. Perhaps Ferret would like the outside world better than their world and never return! The six friends each used their own unique tactics to persuade Ferret to remain in the kingdom. Ferret decided not to go.

As time went on, the seven friends grew closer and closer. They even began to adopt each other's characteristics. Soon Weasel could be seen hiding like Mouse, and Eagle was changing color like Chameleon, and Chameleon was known to be trying to fly. They grew so much alike that life became very confused and the friends lost their own individuality. Life on the farm became perplexing and disorderly, difficult and unhappy as the friends forgot how to be their separate selves.

The other inhabitants on the farm watched this development and sometimes saw the seven friends as one and the same. The being they saw looked different from anything they knew. It walked on two legs, had no wings and no tail, and spoke in a language none of them understood. Instead of living on the land, it lived in a big white house. It was a strange creature and acted in strange ways.

The farm inhabitants tried to tell the seven friends about the creature they had become, but the friends were fighting with one another too much to listen. When Opossum changed color, Chameleon grew angry and told her to make up her mind. When Mouse went hunting, Ferret followed along behind and pestered her to do it the right way. When Fox played dead, Opossum nudged her and said to stop being stupid. The friends were in quite a mess. No one could trust the others' behavior, they couldn't depend on one another, and no one really knew how to act anymore.

One day, the friends saw something shiny, far away across the boundary of the farm. It shimmered and sparkled in the sunlight and beckoned them closer. The friends wondered whether they should go away from the farm to see this fascinating thing. They argued and fought, as had become their habit, until the other farm inhabitants, tired of the constant bickering, encouraged them to go. The friends listened for once, and off they went.

They were so excited they didn't even notice when they crossed the boundary of the farm. The shiny thing was just ahead of them now, and the friends were delirious with anticipation. "It's a mirror! It's a mirror!" they cried. Then, all of a sudden, the mirror disappeared.

Oh, the friends were so disappointed. They wept and wept and then began fighting amongst themselves, trying to decide whether they should go on and try to find the mirror or turn back to the safety of the farm. Eagle said she was going on and for the first time she stretched her wings and soared into the sky. She circled above the group and called down to them, describing how free she felt. She said for them to come along with her to find the mirror. The six on the ground, envying Eagle's freedom, forged ahead into the unknown.

Much to their amazement, the mirror appeared again. With Eagle leading the way, the friends hurried onward. Just before reaching the mirror, they came to a huge hole in the ground. It looked like a bottomless pit. They couldn't go around and they were afraid to go in. Then Fox came up with a solution. She said they should all hold paws and, one at a time, go into the hole. If they stayed together they might get through.

Fox's solution worked. They discovered the hole really did have a bottom and even though it was dark and frightening, they were able to find their way without getting lost. Eagle was waiting for them on the other side and they continued on their journey, enjoying each other's company for the first time in a long while.

The mirror was very close now. Or so it seemed. Every time they drew near, the mirror disappeared and then reappeared a little further away. The friends were getting discouraged. Finally they gave up. Opossum played dead, Chameleon changed color, Mouse hid, Ferret hunted, Weasel told deceitful tales, Eagle flapped uselessly as though she had forgotten all about her new ability to fly. But Fox sat quietly, observing her friends. Instead of being clever, she spoke honestly for once, saying she was exhausted from the effort of trying to find the mirror. In fact, she was also tired of trying to be like someone else when all she really wanted was to be herself. She suggested they gather together to use each one's special qualities and work as a team.

At that moment, the mirror appeared right in front of them. It was a glorious thing, all gilt and gold, and shone with a brilliance so bright the friends turned away from it. They were quite afraid.

Then Mouse, instead of hiding, screwed up her courage and timidly looked toward the mirror. She gasped with delight. When Chameleon heard Mouse, she too looked at the mirror and was pleased with what she saw. Then Opossum, Ferret, Eagle, and Fox cautiously swung around and looked, and they were enthralled.

Weasel was the last to gaze into the mirror, because Weasel was the most afraid. She was more afraid, even, than Mouse. She hid it from the others by being deceitful, but the others knew about Weasel and understood that her deceit mostly fooled only herself.

When Weasel saw the beautiful reflection in the mirror, she wept with relief. The image was not one to be feared but to be embraced. It was the image the other inhabitants of the farm saw and tried to tell them about, a strange creature who walked on two legs, had no wings and no tail, and spoke in a funny language. What was even more amazing was that the friends could understand the words the image was speaking.

"I am the one you have been searching for all your lives. I am all of you combined into a being with strength and character and power and love. I am Opossum who is patient enough to wait for the right moment to act. I am Chameleon who is wise enough to change color when necessary. I am Mouse who is not afraid to hide in perilous times. I am Ferret who is determined enough to pursue truth. I am Weasel whose deceit can be turned into shrewd strategy. I can soar like Eagle whose courage and skill can take her on great journeys of adventure and risk. I am clever and resourceful like Fox, and my wit will carry me into regions of my universe never before explored."

The beautiful creature stepped out of the mirror and spread her arms in an arc encircling the friends. A great wind billowed around them, tossing leaves and petals into the air, and making the atmosphere sparkle with dazzling light. When the wind withdrew, the seven friends were gently and lovingly absorbed into the beautiful being of the strange creature, where they dwelled together in perfect harmony forever after.

The Notes of Gold and Silver

Jan Burg

Once there was a magical child, a child with a great and magical gift. She had a song. Each note of the song was pure gold and silver. Wherever the child went, she sang her song and brought purity, light, and richness.

On her wanderings, she came to a poor kingdom ruled by an evil king and queen. They had been cursed by a wizard who cast cruel spells, so the queen could not laugh and the king could rule only in the dark of the night. Their castle was large and cold.

The queen ruled this kingdom of Everymon, poor as it was, with much pomp and circumstance, while the king stayed quietly in the background, saying little, waiting for the night hours. Then he would prowl the dark corridors, wondering what it meant to be a king.

When the magical child crossed the moat and entered the castle, the king and queen were awed by her and her song. They had never experienced anything like the feelings she brought with her music. They welcomed her into the kingdom and into the castle. Now flowers grew where once the soil was barren. The sun seemed to shine more often. Laughter was heard in the streets and even in the castle. What was once heavy became a burden no longer.

And the music. Beautiful, indescribably glorious music such as had never been heard in the kingdom. Music that illuminated, clarified, and made joyful. It was a wonderful time for the people of the kingdom.

In the castle, the queen, who had surrounded herself with black, snarling dogs, sent the dogs away. The queen, who had worn the darkest of dark glasses, allowed them to slip more and more, so that the colors of her kingdom could be seen. The queen, who had always worn a suit of armor, began to dress in silks and satins.

For the king, it was much the same. He who had walked with a stoop began to stand straight and tall. He who lurked in the corridors at night found he could sleep. He who had once given away his power, slowly and gently reclaimed it and wore his crown proudly.

For two years, it was so. The kingdom prospered. It was as if the notes that fell from the child's lips, though gold and silver and precious themselves, illuminated even greater treasures. There was joy and peace in the land. And then one day, as he was walking in the castle garden, the king encountered a beautiful woman, a stranger.

"I hear that there is a child in your kingdom who sings notes of gold and silver," she said.

"Yes, it's true," the king answered. "The notes act as beacons to greater treasures, some of which we had forgotten existed."

The woman smiled and said she understood that, but what of the notes themselves? Where were they kept?

"Why, what a strange question," the king said. "We have nothing to do with them. But yes, you are right, there should be notes lying about all over."

The woman then explained that she was a queen from another realm, and that her kingdom too had been visited by such a child. "But alas, we paid no attention to the notes, and as the child grew older, she shared her song with others outside the kingdom, making them prosperous. We suffered for it. Our kingdom withered and died because the silver and gold notes were gone. Take warning, oh king." And with that, she smiled mysteriously and disappeared. How could he know that she was the wicked wizard in disguise?

The king was much disturbed. He did not want to believe the beautiful woman, but then again, he did not want his kingdom to wither and die. He grew restless at night, his sleep was disturbed, and once again he wandered the corridors. One night he found himself outside the child's room. Slowly he opened the door and saw that the room was lighted softly by the glow of the gold and silver notes lying about. With one quick motion, hardly thinking about it at all, he reached into the room and took one gold and one silver note. He closed the door and scurried back to his chambers and locked the notes away in a chest.

He decided he would steal a few notes every day, and if what the beautiful woman said was true, he would be able to save the kingdom and his castle, even if the child took her song away. And this is what he did. Each night, he crept into the child's room and took away a note or two. Nobody noticed. Nobody knew. Not even the child knew. She continued to sing her song and the kingdom continued to prosper and the king continued to steal the notes one by one.

Years passed. The kingdom had grown, and so had the child. One day, the child went to the king and queen and said that she had lost some of the notes to the song and her song had become discordant; she must leave the kingdom and search for them. When she found the missing notes and her melody was complete, she would return.

Darkness settled over the old king's heart and he asked, "Are you going to sing your song outside the kingdom?"

"Of course," said the child. "My song is to be sung, but I cannot complete it here. I must leave to find the missing notes."

The queen and king were unhappy at the child's news, but in the king's heart, he rejoiced, for what that beautiful woman had said years ago was true! And his kingdom would not wither and die, for he had kept the gold and silver notes. He did not know that hidden notes cannot make a song.

So the child set out on her journey.

She traveled for years, singing her song, but it was a little discordant and the gold and silver notes did not illuminate as they once had. She searched high and low through distant lands, but try as she might she could not complete her melody. There were times when her melody soared and it felt complete, but then the notes would fade away. It was bewildering to the child. It had been so easy before. What had happened? Where had the notes flown? She sang less and less.

One day, she came upon an old, very poor woman sitting at the base of a huge tree at a crossroads. "Please, child, do you have a song? I am old and ill and have no money, and I have not heard a song in so long," the woman said.

"I seldom sing anymore," said the child. "And my song is not complete. But I can sing you all I have." The child lifted her voice in love and celebration of the woman before her. The magical notes floated into the air, but again, the notes faded away and her song was not complete.

The old woman nodded her head and said, "When I was a young woman, I heard such a song. It was in a kingdom called Everymon."

"But that is where I am from!" cried the child. "I left there to complete my song."

The old woman smiled gently. "You *have* completed your song. You have not found the missing notes because they were lost in that kingdom. They were stolen from you and they are still there."

With the old woman's words, a cloud moved across the sun and the child felt chilled. She had promised to return, but could she go back without the missing notes? Was the old woman speaking the truth? Should she trust this old woman, or should she continue on her journey?

The old woman reached up and took the child's hand. "You deserve to sing your song. You deserve to have the missing notes." She reached into her bag lying in the dust beside her and took out a pair of glasses. "These are special glasses, child. They are to be worn so that one can see the truth. Do not wear them unless you really *want* to see the truth." She reached into her bag again and took out a glass vial. "This is a very special liquid," said the old woman. "You will need it for your journey." Finally, she withdrew a long mirror. "This is to see your self. You will know when to use this mirror."

The child accepted the items from the old woman and turned back for the long journey to return to the kingdom. She had traveled far, and soon she grew weary. She stopped to rest at the junction of many paths. She couldn't decide which path to take, there were so many, going in all different directions. It was bewildering. From a path on her left, there came a very old man. He walked slowly, as if he were in pain.

"I am weary," said the old man in greeting. He slumped to the ground, and the child could see him clearly. He was ill and covered with sores that were weeping and running. He smelled foul from the sores. The child drew back in horror, but when the old man moaned, she was overcome with compassion. This was a dreadful condition to be in. The poor old man needed something to give him strength. She lifted her voice in song. Its melody soared and dipped and wove a blanket over the old man and he slept.

The child pulled the glass vial from her pocket. Perhaps the special liquid the old woman had given her would heal his sores. Slowly she poured the liquid over the sores. In an instant the old man was healed and he awakened to find himself free.

"For years, I have carried those sores," he said, "and now I am well. For your kindness I give you gifts for your journey." He reached into his robe and took out a loaf of bread. "This you will need," he said. "You will also need this," and he handed her a knife. Finally, he handed her a bellows. He smiled gently and began to shrink. He grew smaller and smaller and more and more luminous until at her feet lay a golden object in the dust.

The child put on the glasses of truth that the old woman had given her and she saw that the golden object was one of her missing notes and she saw the truth of her loss of the notes. She ripped the glasses off and threw them to the side of the road. "This is too painful to see!" she cried. She stayed at the crossroads for a very long time.

Finally, she picked up the note and put on the glasses again. She could see the truth of the roads before her and knew which way to go.

A few days later, she walked through fields overgrown with weeds and past cut forests and tumble-down houses where children were crying. In the distance, she saw a castle and with a sense of shock realized that she had come home. This withered, dying kingdom had been her home. What had happened? In this destruction, how could she find her missing notes? Where were the king and queen?

She approached the gates of the castle and found them overgrown with briars. Their stalks were as thick as tree trunks. "How will I ever get through?" she wondered. But then she remembered the gifts of the old man. She pulled the knife out and slashed and separated the gnarled and twisted branches, opening a passageway.

Once inside, however, she felt faint. She nibbled at the loaf of bread, and her strength returned, even greater than before. Now she advanced through the courtyard and into the castle. Everything was dark and abandoned. No music, no laughter, no people! In the main chamber she set down her bundle, resting the mirror against the wall in a dark corner.

It was very cold in the room, so she gathered some of the debris on the floor and tried to light a fire. It did not take well until she used the bellows the old man had given her. As the breath blew out of the bellows, the fire sprang to life and spread over the debris on the floor. It burned everything, and when it had burned out, she saw, mixed in the ashes, a strange object. Picking it up, she brushed it off. Then she put on the glasses and recognized her own heart.

It had been here all this time. And now she could see a glow in the ashes that came from the rest of her missing notes. Her melody was complete! Triumphantly she lifted her voice in song. The notes were pure and sweet and healing.

She glanced up and saw her reflection in the mirror. Why, she was no longer a child. She was a woman! As she continued singing, the notes grew more rich and full and passionate. The song drifted out over the barren fields, through the wretched forests, and into the hearts of all who heard, and the land was healed.

The song was complete and the woman had come home.

The Creation of PMS

Mindy Kauffman

nce upon a time, when the Earth was very young, there was a big decision to be made. All of the men of Earth and all of the women of Earth got together to make this momentous decision. The people gathered in a primordial glen. A woman stepped forward out of the crowd and put forth the idea to be decided upon. She said something like this:

"Today we have come together to decide who among us, the men or the women, will have the honor of giving birth to the children."

There rose and fell a wave of excited speech, a clamoring of hope and enthusiasm. Everyone, men and women alike, yearned for this honor. The men shouted, "We will! We will! We want to do it!" The women asserted, "No! We want to do it, we can do it better!"

The woman who had stepped out of the crowd and become the leader hissed, "Silence!" and the crowd ceased its noise and fell silent. "Since this is such a solemn and important honor," said the leader woman, "and since we all want so dearly to have it bestowed upon us, I propose that there be a contest between the men and the women to see who is most fit for the job."

The crowd murmured and then agreed. "A contest! Yes, a contest!"

Now since both the men and the women wanted to have the honor of giving birth to the children, and neither trusted the other to come up with a fair contest, the task was given to the beasts of the forest.

Brother Bear wanted to see who could build the coziest den, for this was important for the future babies. Sister Cheetah set the task of who could run the longest without tiring. Cousin Squirrel expected the men and women to show their food-gathering and food-storing skills. Brother Otter wanted to see the people express their nurturing skills in the tender rocking rhythms of the ocean. Finally, Sister Owl wanted the contestants to show how they could learn, listen, and remember.

The day of the contest was set. It was a bright and sunny morning. Everyone came early, and hopes and expectations were high. Uncle Lion presided over the contest in his laid-back way. "Okay," Uncle Lion said with a yawn, "all you people line up." The men and the women jostled a bit and lined up, and the Lion continued. "The contest will begin with pairs of men and women working their way through all of the tasks."

Thus began a long, busy, hot day.

The women proved to be the coziest den-builders. (Even the men admitted that!) Next came the food-gathering task, as everyone searched the forest, climbed the trees, and traveled the river banks. Finally the women came back with more nuts, seeds, berries, fish, grains, and other fruits than the men had.

They all broke for lunch.

After lunch the men and the women went into the ocean to play and nurture the Otter pups. The men said, "Gee this feels awkward," and "This is such hard work; couldn't we just do it part-time or once in a while?" The Otters were not impressed. They pronounced the women the winners of their task.

Now it was time to run with Sister Cheetah. At first, the men did very well. They dashed ahead and left the women behind in the dust. But the women kept going, and after a time they caught up with the men and, running steadily on, they passed them. When the women crossed the finish line, the men were nowhere in sight. At last the men dragged into the finish, saying, "Wow! We're pooped! How did you women keep going so long?" Then they collapsed in a heap. The women, having rested for a while, fixed dinner, washed two loads of laundry, and painted each others' toenails. The men, too tired to eat, slept on the floor, and snored.

The next morning, the final part of the contest was to be decided. Sister Owl gave the men and women a lengthy test of learning, listening, and remembering. All of the men and women did very well. They all did so well, in fact, that Sister Owl said there was no difference and this contest was a tie.

Uncle Lion was awakened from his mid-morning nap to proclaim the results. "Ahem," said the Lion, clearing his throat, "although the men have done very well in some areas, it comes to my attention that the women are best-all-round, and I do hereby proclaim them the winners of this contest." The Lion paused to stretch and yawn. "The women," he went on, "will have the honor of giving birth to the children!"

There was an immediate and unhappy protest from the men. "It's not fair!" they complained. "We really wanted to do it and we didn't do so badly in the contest, and we want a compromise!"

Uncle Lion turned and asked the women if they would agree to a compromise. The women, overjoyed with winning the contest, were in a good mood. They said they would listen.

The men proposed that if the women got all the perks of child-bearing—the feelings of new life moving within them, the overwhelming love for the new being, the power of the baby coming forth from their loins, and the tender suckling of the babe at the breast—there had to be a trade-off.

A particularly unpleasant fellow now suggested that during the times the ladies were not with child, they should be visited by a rhythmic outpouring of blood from their bodies—say, every month or so. When this suggestion was met with hostile stares from the women, the unpleasant man replied, "Well, there has to be blood, doesn't there? Where will the baby get its blood if not from you? Are you willing to give up some of your own blood supply?"

He turned, grinning, to the other men, sure that no one would be willing to do such a thing. In those days, of course, they didn't know that the blood could be

replenished. To his surprise, though, the women begrudg-
ingly agreed that this made sense. They said, "All right,
we agree. But let's at least make it a regular experience so
we will know when to expect it. We'll have it come on
schedule with the moon!"

Now the men thought that this compromising
was coming a little too easily and that the women seemed
too anxious and agreeable to this idea. The particularly
unpleasant man whispered amongst his fellow men, the
rhythms of their speech rising and falling. Then he smiled
horribly and spoke up again. "Oh, and one more thing.
When this outpouring of blood occurs, as you say, with
the coming of the full moon ..." his voice trailed off.

"Yes, what then?" asked the women in ago-
nized expectation.

"About a week before this outpouring happens," continued the unpleasant man, "you will tempo-
rarily go insane!" All the men smirked at each other. This
was going to be a good trade-off.

"What will happen to us?" asked the by-now
desperate women. "Oh," said the man, "things like you'll
puff up, you won't be able to sleep at night, you'll be con-
stipated, you'll have headaches, you'll have sore breasts,
you'll cry a lot, you'll worry about things you don't usually
worry about. And you'll howl at the moon!"

The women had to think about this. After much
cloistered deliberation, they returned to the men. The
leader woman stepped forward. "Okay," she said, "we've
decided that being able to give birth to the children is worth

this monthly thing, so we'll compromise and go ahead and do it."

The men were very happy with this. They had won. Or had they?

When the babies came, the men saw the connection and the power the women and the babies had with Nature and the Universe, and they were envious.

And that monthly thing—well, that had been the worst idea of all. Once a month the women did howl at the moon, and sometimes it was bloodcurdling. The men realized that they had cursed themselves as well as the women. They noticed this most often when they were booted out of the cave on a cold, moonlit night and they wandered about, shivering and thinking that maybe, just maybe, they could have struck a better deal.

The Teardrop Coat
Charleen Whitney

nce upon a time, there was a community of beavers who lived deep in the woods. Each family of beavers in the community had its own stream. They were all very traditional beavers, doing what beavers are expected to do: build their dams as their ancestors had for centuries before. But one of the beavers, in one of the families, was different. This young beaver tried hard to be just like her mother and father and brothers and sisters and all her relatives. She wanted to fit in, to be as happy gnawing wood and building dams as they were, but she loved best to lie on the bank and listen intently to the magical sounds of the forest. They filled her senses with the wonder of life.

Her family did not approve of her ways. "Why don't you act like a real beaver?" they would ask. "Why do you lie around and daydream? You should keep busy like we do. There are trees to fell, dams to build, food to gather. What's wrong with you?" Sometimes they laughed at her. "You are too dreamy and too clumsy. You can't do anything right. Not only that, you don't even look like us. Your fur is ugly."

"Mother, Father," the beaver children would say, "Why isn't she like us?"

"Well," the father responded, "we found her under a leaf. That's why she is different. She's not a real beaver." And they would all laugh again.

This would hurt and confuse the female. "But I look like all of you. And isn't it wonderful to dream?" she asked.

"No," her parents told her. "We don't dream, and it's not okay to be different. This is a dangerous, wild forest, and if you want to survive you must be just like us. You must think and act as we do or you could die. There are animals out there who would love to eat you up. Be careful, be like us, work hard, and maybe you'll be all right. Just get any other silly ideas out of your head."

What they said chilled her to the bone. She was freezing. She thought, "I need a coat to warm me and protect my fur. I don't ever want to feel this cold again." So she fashioned a coat out of teardrop-shaped leaves. "This is very pretty," she thought. "I will never be cold again."

Her family admired her coat. "Now you've finally done something sensible," said her father. "Just don't ever take it off because your fur is not as pretty as ours and it embarrasses the family."

So the female wore her coat and tried to be just like all the other beavers. She learned how to swim effortlessly through the water. She learned to fell the trees, to build the dam and house. She learned to gather food and hunt. She was so busy all the time, she no longer would lie on the bank and dream. "I guess they were right," she told herself. "I should be like them. I know I'll be happier."

But occasionally, when no one was around, she couldn't resist stopping and listening to the forest. She would even open her coat and feel the breeze against her fur. "It would be nice to take off this coat, but I know I need it to protect me," she thought. "And my fur is so dull and matted beneath it. I always thought it was beautiful, but it's ugly, just as the other beavers said." So she kept the coat on and sometimes added a pretty feather or flower to it. Often she felt so cold she wrapped the coat snugly around her, grateful for its protection.

One day she met a male beaver who had wandered over to their stream. "He is handsome," she thought. "I think I'll take him for a mate. We'll build our own dam, have children, dream together, and of course, live happily ever after." They joined together and one day, she asked him shyly, "Would you like to see my fur under this coat? I could take off my coat for you."

"No," he said. "I don't want to see your fur. I have much more important things to do, like finding trees to cut down."

Her feelings were hurt, but she convinced herself it didn't matter. She thought, "He might laugh anyway and his breath would feel cold against my fur. It's better this way, I'm sure."

So off they went in search of their own stream. Finally they found the perfect spot. The beaver said to herself, "I will try to remember everything I've been taught.

I will work hard and build a beautiful house of sticks. Everyone will be proud of me. I will make my mate happy."

Before long she had two children. She felt a love for them that she had never known possible. They were the most wonderful gifts she had ever received. She thanked the creator every day for these children. She would say to the insects and the birds and the four-leggeds, "Look, look at my beautiful babies. Are they not perfect? They will grow to be strong yet gentle and loving, wise yet humble. They will be exactly what they need to be. I am blessed to have them. I will be the best parent I can be." And the animals all agreed; these were special children.

By this time her mate had grown weary of life on their stream. "I need more room," he said. "I need to see other beavers besides you and the children. I'm sure you understand."

She did try to understand. After all he was the head of the family, and his needs came first. So off he went, wandering around the forest, leaving the female with her babies. At first she was frightened. "What if I can't find food? What if the dam breaks? What if we're attacked by other animals? Who will protect us?" Yet, over the years, she found that she was capable of taking care of herself and her children.

"You keep doing what you are doing," said her parents. "Your mate is just being like all the other male beavers, so it's all right."

Gradually the beaver noticed that her coat was becoming heavier and heavier. All this time she had been adding more new teardrop leaves and decorating the coat with feathers until it weighed her down. Everyone admired her coat, but it had grown uncomfortable. "I hardly remember what my fur looks like," she thought. "It has been so many years since I let the breeze blow against my fur. I loved this coat. It has protected me. I decorated it so attractively, but now I feel as though it is suffocating me."

She asked her mate, "Will you help me take off this coat, so we both can see what my fur looks like? I think I would feel better without it."

"Absolutely not," he replied. "I like that coat and I don't want to see your fur. Do not take it off." Her parents and family chimed in. "Leave it on. If you take the coat off you might act different again. You might start lying by the stream, daydreaming instead of being a proper beaver. You will embarrass us."

The female was sad. "Why, I can barely swim anymore. I can't run, my house of sticks is falling apart, and I can't work on the dam. My children might get hurt if the dam collapses. Not only that, I want to show my children my fur. Oh, and how I want to see it myself. To feel the breeze against my fur. To be free." But she was afraid, and somehow she no longer knew how to remove the coat. So she said to her children, "I'll make you coats just like mine so you can be protected."

"No," they cried. "We are not like you. We don't want coats. We don't need them. Why don't you take yours off?"

"Because I need the protection," their mother replied.

But she thought to herself, "My children are happy without coats. I don't want them to stop running and swimming and feeling the breeze against their fur. I remember the time when I didn't need a coat, so very long ago. It felt good to be without it, no matter what my family says. I must do something, because soon I will suffocate to death. My children will not have a mother, and they will never know what I was truly like. I want them to see me. Even if my fur is dull and matted now, I don't care. It's who I am."

About this time, when the beaver was feeling desperate, she met a very wise and loving bird who became her friend. "That's an interesting coat you're wearing. Why does it look like teardrops?" she said.

"Oh, that's just a coincidence, I'm sure," said the beaver.

"Would you like to take it off and come fly with me?" the bird asked.

"I don't think that's possible. You see, I'm a beaver. I can't fly. I can't even run or swim anymore because of my heavy coat."

"Well, maybe you can't fly, but you could run and swim again," the bird said. "Why don't you try? Take off your coat."

"My fur is so ugly. Maybe I don't even have any fur left. And if I remove the coat, I might die from the cold," said the beaver.

"Try it. Trust me and trust yourself. I'm not saying it won't be uncomfortable for a while, since you are no longer used to feeling the breeze or the water or the grass against your fur, but you will not die. And if you leave on the coat, you will surely die," the bird said. "Why don't you start by removing one teardrop leaf at a time. That way you can learn to feel again, little by little."

The beaver said, "I am willing to try."

Her mate was outraged. "I will not allow you to remove your coat," he said.

Her parents were outraged. "You cannot do this. You will not survive," they said.

But she knew she must. She knew she wanted to. So she left the stream in search of a place where she could slowly remove her coat, and where she could teach her children about life. She wanted a place where she could lie quietly on the bank and remember who she was. She wanted a place where she could see, smell, and hear the sounds of life again. She felt frightened and alone, but knew deep inside that she must take this journey not only for herself but for her children.

A few friends and a few family members helped her along the way as she slowly began to remove pieces of her coat. When she found her place by a quiet stream, she settled down. She would look at her reflection in the water and wonder who she was. At first she didn't recognize herself. Sometimes she would like what she saw, and other times she wouldn't. Sometimes she was tempted to put the coat back on. Many times she felt naked and vulnerable without the coat. But with the encouragement of her friend the bird, she decided it was worth feeling cold once in a while, because without her heavy coat she could hold her children. She could feel their heartbeats.

Slowly the beaver's dull fur began to shine again. She felt lighter and stronger. She wanted to build a new dam and home of her own design, and she did. She let herself dream. And she found to her delight that she was able to run and swim again.

She still has a few pieces of the teardrop coat, but they do not weigh her down anymore. They help remind her of where she's been and occasionally provide her with the small amount of protection she feels she needs. Her fur has grown back shiny, thick, and beautiful. She can again lie on the bank of her stream and listen to the magical sounds of nature, and she is at peace.

The Special Gift

Sharon Patterson

nce upon a time, many years ago, a child was born. The young mother and father were over-joyed with their beautiful baby girl. The mother was especially pleased, because she knew what was in store for this blessed child.

Every afternoon just before naptime and every evening before bed, the mother would hold the child and rock her, and as she rocked she told her of her heritage. She said, "My precious little daughter, you are no ordinary child. You are endowed with wondrous wealth, a very special gift from your motherline. When you are older, you will understand this great gift we have for you."

For years the mother told her daughter about the gift that was so important, and the daughter began to wonder when she would ever see it. "When, Mama? When will I be old enough?" she asked.

And the mother always smiled and answered, "Later, my dear. When you are ready."

As the child grew, the answer changed. It became, "You shall know soon. Very soon."

When the child reached school age, she thought of herself as a big girl now, yet still she had not learned about the special gift. Then, at last, on the night before she was to go off to her first day at school, the time arrived.

The mother sat in her rocking chair, and the child sat on a stool at her feet, as they always did. The mother stroked her daughter's long, silky hair, lovingly tied back with a red ribbon, and said, "Before you venture out into the world to school, I have a story to tell you about your gift."

The child wiggled in excitement. Finally she would learn about her gift! Would it be a beautiful doll or a wonderful toy? Or something she couldn't imagine? She held her breath, ready to listen.

"You are blessed, my daughter," the mother said. "On the day you were born, your mothers before you, or Goddesses, as I know them, decided to give you a special gift. That gift has been with you every day, all day long, since the day you were born."

The girl was puzzled. Slowly she said, "But Mama, I don't remember getting any special gift. Where is it? Have you been hiding it?"

Her mother smiled. "Soon you will see it and claim it," she said. "In fact, you can claim it this night, if you wish."

The child jumped to her feet. "Yes, I want it now!"

"Come with me to the window."

They went to the window and looked out at the clear night sky, and the mother pointed out a bright glittering star, just overhead. She said, "There is your special gift from your motherline. That star is yours, and no one can take it from you. You will always live in the light of that star; it represents the love of your motherline. The love behind your star will shine through and comfort you when you are sad or upset. It will twinkle when you are happy, guide you when you are lost, and protect you always."

The child was delighted at the thought of that bright shiny star being hers. But could she really talk to it and be protected by it? She wasn't sure she believed this story. It sounded like one of the many fairy tales her mother read to her.

"How can my star guide and protect me?" she asked. "I don't understand."

The mother pointed to the sky. "Do you see that other star, just beyond the Big Dipper? That is your grandmother Cecily. And that one over there is your grandmother Rose, and that one over there is your great grandmother Emily." The mother continued to point to and name the stars. When she was through, she said, "Now I want to show you your treasure. First, ask the Goddesses in the heavens for your star. Remember to say please!" she added teasingly.

The daughter reached her hand to the sky and said, "Please, Goddesses in heaven, may I please, please have my star now?"

She stretched and strained to see if her star moved. Disappointed, she turned back to her mother. "I knew this was just a fairy tale you made up. My star never moved, it's still up there! I don't believe you."

Her mother smiled. She knew this independent, strong daughter of hers would need proof. But all she said was, "You'll see soon. Now get ready for bed, and I'll come to tuck you in and kiss you goodnight."

The child did as she was told. She brushed her teeth and washed her face, brushed her hair and undressed and got into her nightgown. As she climbed into bed, she murmured, "Mama, you shouldn't have fooled me." And she began to cry. The mother came in and sat on the bed, where the pretty flowered quilt was folded down. She reached her arms toward her daughter, but the little girl turned away. "You shouldn't have fooled me. I always used to believe you, and now I don't."

"My dear, reach under your pillow."

The child was suspicious, but slowly she moved her hand under the pillow. She felt something warm and smooth and solid. She closed her hand around it and pulled it out. She opened her clutching hand and there, to her amazement, lay a beautiful star, glowing bright against her small palm.

She ran to the window and looked up at the sky. There was the star that her mother said was hers, still shining against the dark. "How could that be? I'm holding my star here in my hand."

The mother went to the window and put her arm around her daughter. She said, "Your star is in your hand. And the one in the heavens is also yours. You can put this one in your pocket, on a chain around your neck, in a box for safekeeping, or anywhere you like. The one in the heavens is there so you will always know you are loved and are not alone. That is the gift of the Goddesses. That is the gift that will protect you and guide you as long as you believe in yourself, love yourself, and live your life true to your heart. That, my child, is your blessing from your motherline. This gift will make you powerful in fulfilling your dreams, and it will bring you peace and love. Don't ever doubt yourself or the Goddesses. They will be with you always."

The little girl listened in wonderment, and then she slept and the next day went off to school.

Over the years she often thought of that evening when her mother showed her the Goddesses' special gift. To this day, whenever she has doubts or questions, if she feels afraid or wants to share her thoughts, she holds her special star and talks to the Goddesses. She knows she is always loved and safe.

Star Journeys
and Crystal Dreams

Jo Gille Aldrich

nce upon a time, in a land where illusion was more prized than reality, a girl-child was called to birth. The other presence with her on the birth journey from the stars was stilled and the girl went alone on baby feet to gaze down long roads and didn't know why. She watched the coyotes playing in the winds and the blackbird with orange-seared wings in the drooping willows, songs of molten silver pouring from his throat. She listened to the call of the night train haunting the lonely valleys and wondered why she kept vigil. She dreamed dreams of dusky hills with grasses rippling and swaying, parting as unseen feet slipped past her, and she didn't know why. She heard far-off Gypsy music and didn't know that it came from the Gypsy spirit woven into her family's tapestry.

The little girl fell ill and feverish. Her mother grew frightened when the girl, in her illness, called on forces to come to her aid, mystical and ancient forces the mother had only heard whispered of before this time. The child cried for the Gypsy and for the lost one—the twin who had begun the journey from the stars with her but did not live to complete it.

The girl recovered from her illness and grew into a woman, and messages came to her in dreams. The powers cautioned her and she was afraid, but the dreams lured her, a reluctant voyager to strange lands. She wandered bitter streets and tried on other souls. She tasted the coldness of despair and the hopelessness of anticipated death. She searched for the twin spirit that was lost at birth. She heard Gypsy music calling and she yearned to follow it.

The woman married and bore a daughter with hair the color of the moon and a son with eyes like the sea. Some said that it was their Gypsy legacy, brought to them by their mother. The boy looked with clear eyes into her mind and the woman was afraid. Her husband noticed the restlessness in the woman and her children and was afraid of the Gypsy.

The woman hid her restlessness and busied herself with daily cares and worries. She dream-journeyed no more. The children and the wild Gypsy spirit watched and waited for a long time.

One day when she was alone in a quiet place, the woman dreamed again. In her dream, the Gypsy appeared, laughing. The woman asked the Gypsy questions, the great questions of life. And so the gift of many trials was placed before her.

"This is an ugly gift. I don't want it," said the woman.

"You have asked the questions, and so you must take it," the Gypsy said. "There is a treasure at the end of each trial that can be claimed only by you."

The woman asked what the treasures were. She was told only that each one would make her stronger in a different way. Reluctantly the woman accepted the gift of many trials. She awakened from her dream, and the trials began. They were harsh and unrelenting, and many times she felt that they would defeat her, yet she passed through them and prevailed. Along the way she collected her treasures without knowing what to do with them.

She counted the treasures, put them in a pile, and grew more restless than ever. She thought to herself, I need to travel. There are more discoveries to be made. Surely that won't be bad. I will hurt no one.

She went to the place where the trees whispered together. There were many animals who knew her. She grew still and listened to the animals and the trees and remembered a little of the magic of her early star journeys. Gently, gently, the peacefulness of the place entered into the woman, and she slept and dreamed of a place of great learning, a place of peace and knowledge and love.

When she awoke, the woman gathered up her treasures. She would go to the place of learning and ask the Wise Elders what they meant and why she was still unhappy and restless.

Some people told her she should not go and tried to stop her. They said she should be glad of what she already had and they urged her to share her treasures with them. This saddened the woman, but she knew they had to find their own treasures. The voices were shrill and insistent. They said she was selfish and wicked and what would become of them?

The woman's only answer was that it was late and the path was growing dark. Her daughter said nothing but slipped her hand into her mother's. Her son said, "I will walk a little way with you," and he fell into step beside his sister and their mother.

The Gypsy spirit laughed and sang songs to the goblins and danced on striped moon paths ahead of them.

The woman wanted to save her treasures and present them to the Wise Elders, but, one by one, she used them to light the path she followed. Patience, humility, compassion, love, connection—all were needed to find the way.

The woman's daughter slipped away to follow her own journey. The son continued on a little longer, but soon he too could go no further. The woman's husband watched from below as she crossed many chasms, and it was only the Gypsy who paced with her along the rim. It was only the Gypsy beside her as the woman finally stood, shabby, weary and humbled before the Elders.

"I am here," she said to them, "but I have nothing to give you. My treasures are all gone. I have nothing left but questions."

"Questions," said the Elders. "Questions can be gifts, too, but first you must take the most important journey of all for your final treasure."

"And what is that?" asked the woman. She was suddenly afraid.

"The one you have been avoiding all your life," was the reply.

"But I don't know what that is," cried the woman. "Please help me." The Elders smiled and shook their heads.

The woman turned away, sad and bewildered. Where was she to start this journey? Hadn't she done enough already?

The Gypsy watched and listened and cursed as the woman tried on lives and discarded them with feverish hands and finally, exhausted, lay down to rest. She slept and dreamed.

"Dance with me," said the Gypsy to the woman on her dream-journey. "Come dance with me." The woman placed her hand in the Gypsy's hand. They danced in an amethyst cavern, and their steps echoed as they whirled faster and faster, in a mad dervish of discord.

"No more," said the woman. "I am weary. I cannot dance."

"Come with me," said the Gypsy. The woman followed the Gypsy along a path of smoke. Gently, here and there, crystals like stars sang and fell silent. The Gypsy stopped and pointed.

The figure standing before them turned its head and looked at the woman. The crystals sang softly and their light flowed over the being in front of her. "What do you see?" asked the Gypsy.

The woman said, "I see that the quest is the answer."

"Now look at me," said the Gypsy. "What do you see?"

Lost memories stirred. Her hopes and dreams rose before her. "Live the quest," she said simply.

The Gypsy laughed and whirled her back through the stars, and she returned to the Elders to stand in the truth of her dream-journey.

"You have returned," said the Wise Ones. "Can you tell us what you have found as your greatest treasure?"

The woman smiled. "I have found myself."

The Garden Patch

Nancy Anderson

ith the warm sun beaming down upon her, the young woman lovingly tended her garden. There were three flowers of her very own in the garden, and she saw that they had everything they needed. She planted them in rich soil and fed and watered them well. She cared for her garden every day. And she cherished each flower's very presence.

Each flower was unique in some special way. The flower she had planted first was a big, tall plant. He was strong and constantly striving to dominate the other flowers. The second flower was small and weak, and although he too was beautiful, he was jealous of the bigger, stronger flower. The third and last flower was a wild seedling that grew where she pleased. There was no controlling this plant, she was always in charge.

Despite their differences, the flowers seemed to grow in harmony. The Mother Gardener was proud. She had provided perfect placement for all three.

One special day in early spring, as the young woman was weeding and watering her flowers, she noticed something new, something completely unexpected. Much to her surprise, over in the corner a tiny stem was making its way out of the soil. Gently the Mother Gardener nudged the green stem and inquired, "Are you a new flower to my family? I do not remember planting you. How could you possibly be here?" The little stem remained silent, not ready to let her identity be known.

The three flowers in the garden leaned toward the stem and asked each other, "Who could this intruder be? We did not ask for another flower in *our* garden. How could our gardener do this to us? This extra flower will drink some of our water. It will want to use our soil and our air and our sunshine. We do not want it."

Despite their wishes for the green sprout to go away, it did just the opposite. Slowly and steadily, in its corner by the fence, the green stem grew and made her way through the soil while the three other flowers and the gardener watched. From the stem a bit of green unfurled. But where was the flower? It was not to be seen. The plant was not a flower. It was a leaf. An undeveloped leaf, yet to unfold.

The Mother Gardener was thrilled. "Oh my, you are a leaf! You are so different. I now have three flowers and one leaf! You will stay right here in the garden, where you will always be safe." Then the gardener put down her trowel and said, "Now I must go away, for I have traveling to do. I have paid someone to come care for my flowers and leaf. She will bring you water and food and keep you safe while I am gone. Goodbye, dear garden." And she was gone.

The three flowers nodded on their stalks. "Hey you, Leaf!" they called. "Just who do you think you are?

We are the flowers of this garden and you are not welcome here. You are different and we do not want you. Who ever heard of a leaf growing right out of the soil? You can't be a real leaf, because if you were, you would be attached to a tree!" They jeered at her, and Leaf had no answer. She looked up at the beautiful blue sky above and was amazed by the wonder of the world. She was eager to grow and become what she could be.

But the flowers didn't want her to grow. They said, "We want you to know that you are going to turn into a flower, or we're going to make you go away." Then the wild flower piled soil in her petals and threw it on the leaf. Her brother flowers laughed and told the wild one she was wasting her time. There was no possible way that weak little leaf could grow, they told her. There was no threat of that at all.

Once in a while the Mother Gardener returned to the garden. At those times she always admired the flowers' beauty and commented on the difference of her leaf. On one of those visits, Leaf gathered her courage and told Mother Gardener how unhappy she was. "I try to be friendly," she said. "I am quiet and out of the way, and still my brother and sister flowers do not want me. They say horrible things to me and while I am trying to grow, they throw soil on me so I cannot. Will you help me grow, Mother Gardener? I want to reach the sky."

Mother Gardener was surprised and bothered that her little leaf was so upset. "It's just your imagination," she assured Leaf. "Your brother and sister flowers love you very much, and you must love them too. But just to be sure that you are safe from any flying soil, I will move you to a far corner of the garden patch." And she did. Before she went away, the gardener planted her leaf in a quiet, secure place with lots of shade.

It didn't make any difference. Leaf could still hear the hurtful words. And they did hurt. She was glad to be safe, but at times she felt awfully lonely. Her sister flower, the wild aggressive one, grew to become a tall and glorious sunflower. A sunflower that continually strived to block the sun from getting to the still-folded leaf.

When Mother Gardener returned from yet another trip, Leaf spoke up. She said, "Mother Gardener, I appreciate all you have done. But I need more. Here I am in my corner, not hurting anyone, trying to grow, and the flowers get in my way and try to stop me. I feel trapped down here!"

"Don't be ridiculous," Mother Gardener answered. "You know they love you and would not hurt you. You are too sensitive. Besides, it won't be long until those flowers will be grown and off living in their own gardens. Then it will be just you and me, and you can grow as much as you wish."

Mother Gardener was perfectly right. The brother and sister flowers grew up and left the garden, and Leaf was alone, with the whole garden to herself. As the years went by, Mother Gardener didn't go away any more. She stayed in the garden and carefully watered her little leaf and kept her packed tightly with fresh soil—not to help her grow, but to keep her safe. Much to the mother's dismay, though, Leaf did start to grow. Mother Gardener did not want this. This was her baby, her precious little leaf. She wanted her to stay small and simple to be safe. She must be safe.

Every time Leaf began to unfold, Mother Gardener was there to stop her. Carefully tucking the unfolded bit back in, Mother Gardener would scold, "Don't you know you are not allowed to do that? You might get hurt!" The little leaf was discouraged. She wondered when she would ever be allowed to grow.

One day, as Leaf sat in the garden watching other leaves freely swaying on their tree in the wind, she wilted in despair. Oh, how badly she wanted to grow. She too wanted to be a fully developed, beautiful, unfolded leaf.

She heard a kindly voice above her. She looked up through the fluttering green leaves and saw that the large and grand tree was looking down at her. "Hello, little Leaf," Mister Tree said.

Leaf began to talk. She told the tree how much she admired him, and that she thought he had the nicest position on earth.

Mister Tree fluttered his leaves for a moment, and then he asked, "Well, then, why don't you become a tree just like me?"

Leaf smiled and responded, "Oh, I could never be a tree. My mother says that I must stay safe. If I became a tree, someone might try to chop me down. No, I couldn't do that."

Despite her denial, Leaf began to think about it. And she decided to figure out a way to break free from the garden.

When Mother Gardener heard this, she was angry. "I don't know what makes you think you could become a tree! Don't be ridiculous. You belong right here. Only very smart leaves can be trees."

With this, Leaf knew what she had to do. She threw herself into learning, trying to become smart enough to become a tree. Now when Mother Gardener came into the garden, Leaf was too busy to receive her care. Instead, she was filling her brain and emptying her heart. As the years passed, the distance between Mother Gardener and Leaf grew. The mother came by now and then, but she soon said she had to be on her way. Leaf missed her mother. She wanted her mother there when she finally became that tree. She wanted her mother to be proud.

At last Leaf decided that she was finally smart. Smart enough to become a tree. All she had to do was do it. So she went to work, stretching every root and sprouting every limb, trying to start her tree.

One afternoon, as she was working at growing a tree, Mother Gardener came by, and a special thing happened. Leaf was tired. She had stretched her roots all day, and one lonely root became uncovered with soil. Leaf thought that the sun might dry it out, and so she asked for Mother Gardener's help. "Would you please cover that root with soil? It would help me so much."

Mother Gardener reached over and gently

placed the new root under the ground. When she was done, she gave it water. And then she smiled, for Mother Gardener and Leaf both knew that these roots were going to cause her to be the tree that Leaf had always wanted to be.

Many years later, Mother Gardener was in need of rest. She had grown old and tired. She was no longer able to care for a garden patch. She couldn't feed or water the flowers and leaves; she had only love to give. As she wandered into the garden and sat on a bench, she looked up and smiled. The sun was bright, but the bench was perfectly placed in the shade of a most glorious and wonderful tree, a tree that grew not from physical care of the hands, but love of the heart. Leaf stood tall and had an endless supply of shade to give.

The Cloth That Had No Purpose

Jeanne Christensen Benjamin

nce upon a time, in a land far beyond the stars, there lived the beautiful Goddess Ella and her soulmate No-Ella. Ella was lovely. Her gown was the color of moonlight and her dark hair flowed like a river, over her shoulders and down in waves where it fell in a pool at her feet. No-Ella was her beautiful opposite. He wore a hooded cloak of azure blue so deep it seemed as if the ocean swept around him when he moved. His hair was a brilliant white, circling his face like a halo. Light glittered from him in a thousand tiny sparkles. The Goddess and her soulmate spent their days in harmony, enjoying their lives of beauty and love.

So happy was Ella, she decided to weave a cloth that reflected the joy of their life together. After many hours of intricate work her weaving was done, and she held up the cloth for No-Ella to admire. The pattern of the cloth was magnificent. She had woven into it her own dark hair, his light, the deep color from his cloak, and the radiance of her gown. She had sewn sparkles from his cloak in each corner. The cloth glowed with a magical beauty.

Suddenly, as she lifted the cloth, a strong wind gusted by and blew it from her hands. Ella cried out, and No-Ella reached to catch it. It was too late. The cloth fluttered away, carried by the wind. They watched it sail among the stars until it was gone from view, floating in a silent, steady descent.

As luck would have it, the wind carried the cloth to the house of a farmer and dropped it through the kitchen window, where it landed at the farmer's feet. He had been working hard in his orchard and was hot and tired, and when he saw the cloth he picked it up to wipe the sweat from his brow. But the cloth was so delicate, so spangled with sparkles, it was no use. The farmer tossed it onto the kitchen table and went back to his work in the orchard.

His wife, working hard in the kitchen as she did every day, noticed the cloth on the table. Exclaiming over its beauty, she dropped her broom and snatched up the cloth and ran to her mirror. Before the mirror she draped the cloth around her shoulders, tied it around her neck, tucked it into her belt, fastened her hair with it. No matter what she did, it didn't look right to her. With a heavy sigh, she folded the cloth neatly, straightened the corners, and smoothed the wrinkles. She placed it in her drawer, closed it, and went back to her broom. The cloth lay in the dark, with no one to enjoy its beauty for a long, long time.

One day the son of the household came to his mother and asked for a cloth to polish his hunting gun. She had used all her rags for scrubbing and had none to give him, and then she remembered the pretty cloth in the drawer. She pulled it out and gave it to him. The son sat on a bench by the back door and began to rub the barrel of his gun with the cloth. At first he thought it was going to do a good job, but when he saw that the funny little sparkles on the cloth scratched the gun, he became very angry. He threw the cloth down on the dirt, stamped on it with his boot, and marched off.

That night two mice scampered by, looking for a cozy place to sleep. The cloth looked just right. They jumped on it, pushed it this way and that, and settled in to sleep. It didn't take long to see that the cloth wasn't big enough for two of them. Soon they jumped up again and ran off to find a bigger nest.

The next morning, the hired man came in from the orchard where he had been working. He sat on the bench to rest and leaned his head against the wall, and as he surveyed the orchard on the other side, he noticed a tree with a branch so heavily laden with fruit it was almost ready to break. He glanced down and saw the cloth at his feet. He picked it up, walked over to the tree with the cracking branch, and tied the cloth tightly around it. He knotted it hard. One knot, two knots, and a few of the cloth's threads ripped, but it held the branch up.

The sun beat down and the wind blew. The cloth faded and became tattered at the edges. Dust covered all the sparkles. The fruit on the tree grew larger and heavier, and the branch creaked with the weight. More threads tore. The cloth would not last much longer.

From far away, the Goddess Ella felt all that

was happening to her creation, and she wept. A few of her tears fell on the cloth, and then a few more, and then a shower. Soon the drops washed the dirt away, and the sparkles shone brightly again.

After the refreshing rain, when everything smelled clean and new, the hired man's little girl decided to go for a walk. As she strolled through the orchard, a shiny flash caught her eye. She spied the cloth, still tied in the tree. She was so taken with it that she worked and worked to untie the knots until she worked it free. She tucked it into her pocket and ran to show her mother.

That night the little girl spread the cloth carefully on the table by her bed and gazed at it for a long time. She fell asleep enjoying its beauty.

Later, while the girl was dancing in dreamland, the moon rose high and full in the sky. At just the right moment, the moon's luminous beams shone through the window. Light reflected off the sparkles and shot joyfully back into the sky. Past the smiling moon, it sailed through the stars and traveled on as fast as light can go, headed homeward.

Goddess Ella and No-Ella felt it coming. They looked up just in time to catch the reflection in each other's eyes. No-Ella smiled into Ella's shining eyes and saw the sparkles from his cloak dancing, and they were both content once again.

The Lioness
Linda

O n the vast savannah all seems tranquil. It is not. Beyond the magnificent swaying grass, at the edge of the jungle, the hunters are lurking. In the distance, the mother Lioness is hurrying her children to safety. She is thankful that she remembered the cave. She had been so afraid that she had forgotten the way. But why did she doubt herself? She has traveled this path for many a year with her mate and the others of the pride. Did she have doubts because now she is the leader, solely responsible for her precious cubs? She is no longer a follower, helping the others along.

How could the others turn away from her when she needed them the most? Why did they ostracize her when her mate is the coward? She did not have control over his actions. She did not advise him to let himself be captured rather than fight the hunters. She is no coward. She has just made this long and frightful trek on her own— that should prove something.

She will not dwell on this matter any further. She has just made a marvelously brave journey and she will begin anew. What does she have to fear? Hurt feelings and loneliness, yes, but she has her children to raise.

The Lioness is now far from the hunters, she

and her cubs are safe. She herself is the hunter. She will provide for her children as she always has in the past. And there will be one less mouth to feed—his. Actually, she begins to wonder, just what did he ever do for us? Nothing. All he did was reign away the day in the sunshine and groom himself ever so carefully. She catered to his every need. She provided for the family and often for others in the pride. She cared for their gallant children. The Lioness has done all of this herself.

Yes, she is more powerful than he, more intelligent, and certainly far more organized. She will build her own pride, and it will be the strongest and smartest in the land. And if one day a beautifully handsome lion walks her way, she will decide his worth, and she will decide if he may join her pride.

The Powerful Mother

Tamera Zuber

Long, long ago in a far-off place, there lived a girl named Sara. Sara knew she was very special. She must be, because her mother was always telling her that she was not like other people. "We are different," the mother would say. "We are a family of power and wealth. We are not like the common people."

After Sara's father died and left them with even more riches, her mother told her she should always hold herself above others and remember that she was much better than they were. As she grew older, Sara held on to her mother's words. She had few friends, and she never allowed anyone to come close. Like a princess locked in a tower, she had all that money could buy but was isolated and alone, and finally felt very lonely. Something was missing. Something felt empty.

She could not tell her mother about this feeling, but as she looked out at the world from her lonely tower, it became unbearable. Something had to be done.

One night, after she was sure her mother was asleep, Sara crept away. She walked the quiet roads until she came to a village. The cottages there were small, and the doors were closed, but each had a candle in the window, and Sara could see the people inside and hear their voices. In the first cottage, a family sat around a table, finishing their evening meal. "How is your painting going, Jacquelyn?" the woman asked. "Not very well, Mama," the girl answered with a sigh. "I'm working on a landscape and I can't get the exact shade of green I want. Maybe I'm not such a good artist after all."

Why, that's just like me, Sara thought. I want to be an artist, and I have trouble mixing colors.

In the next house, she could see a boy lying on the hearth, staring into the fire. An old man with a pipe sat in a rocker beside him. "What are you dreaming of, boy?" the man asked. "I'm dreaming of the faraway places I want to see," the boy answered. "I'll sail a ship around the world."

Me, too, Sara thought. I want to travel everywhere.

In the window of the third house, a young woman and man were arguing. "Let's go dancing," the man said. "Come on, Louise, it will be fun." Louise shook her head and said, "No, no, I can't dance. I'm afraid to. Everyone will make fun of me. And I don't know anyone."

She's afraid like me, Sara thought. I bet she's lonely, too.

She continued down the street, and in every window she saw people who talked as she did, felt as she did, and had the same dreams and hopes. When she returned home and climbed wearily into bed, her thoughts were full of what she had seen.

The next night and the next and for many nights

after that, she left home and went to the village and watched the people. She began to feel that she knew them. She cared about Jacquelyn and Louise and the boy who wanted to travel; she wanted them to be happy. One night as she reached the end of the street and was about to turn back, a voice called her. "Sara!"

Startled, Sara peered into the shadows. Who was calling her, who knew her name? "Sara, don't be afraid," the voice said. "I'm over here."

Slowly she walked to the last cottage, the only one without a candle in the window. An old woman sat on the porch; Sara could just see her wrinkled skin and smile in the moonlight.

"I've been watching you, Sara," the old woman said. "I have seen you come here night after night. What have you learned from your visits?"

Sara didn't feel the least afraid of this strange woman who somehow knew her name. "I think I have learned that other people aren't so very different from me after all. They have the same feelings I do. And I care about them."

The old woman smiled. "Good. It is time for you to leave your tower, and go into the world with what you have learned." Slowly she stood, leaning on her cane, and went into her tiny house and closed the door.

The next morning, Sara told her mother she was going away. "You cannot leave me!" her mother cried. "I forbid you to go."

But Sara was firm. "I have to do this, Mother.

I must go out into the world. Please give me your blessing."

"Never. If you go, you cannot come back, and I will never forgive you."

Saddened, Sara packed her things and left. As she walked away in the sunshine, leaving the tower behind, a great weight lifted from her shoulders, and the empty feeling was gone. The villagers welcomed her, and she began a new and fulfilling life. Now her only sadness came when she thought of her mother, and every night she prayed for her mother's happiness.

A year passed. One day a messenger knocked on the door of Sara's little house. She recognized him. He was one of her mother's servants. "Please come," he said. "Your mother is very ill. She has been pining for you, and we fear she will die if she cannot see you."

Sara immediately threw a cape over her shoulders and stepped into the carriage the servant had brought.

In the big, forbidding house, Sara entered her mother's room and saw her lying in bed, thin and still. Softly she took her mother's hand. "I love you, and I've always been sorry for the way we parted," Sara said.

"Why did you leave me?" her mother whispered, as a tear rolled down her cheek.

"Don't you know it was because of you?" Sara asked. "You were so powerful, you set the example and gave me the strength and courage to search for what I believed in and what was most important to me."

The powerful mother smiled, and in her face,
Sara saw again the old woman of the village.

The Living Pond

Jeanne Christensen Benjamin

s is always the way in the grand plan, a small but lovely little pond of water was formed in a valley just over the next hill. Although it was only a tiny body of water, wonderful things happened there. Above and below its surface, lush and magical plant life flourished in blooms of delicate texture and fragrance. Vines twisted and turned through the water in intricate and complicated patterns. Green foliage snuggled close to the water's edge as if to embrace the pond in a mother's loving arms. All kinds of living things thrived. Fish darted here and there, exploring, looking, and feeding. Bugs of sparkling colors jumped and flew from plant to flower to water in a busy parade of activity. At twilight, frogs gathered to make music. They were so fat and richly green they looked like living emeralds scattered about to decorate the pond's edge. It was peaceful and perfect.

One day a loud rumbling could be heard, far away but getting closer. From over the hill, a dark figure appeared and approached with heavy and purposeful strides. Coming to the water's edge, the figure stopped and glared. This pond was in the path that was, of course, the most direct way to the destination. The figure looked around, saw a heavy log nearby, and lifted it and flung it roughly into the pond, where it fell with a great splash. Great ripples of water spilled out, drowning the grass. The bugs flew quickly away, the plants were torn up by their delicate roots, and the fish hid deep down as far as they could go into the mud. The music was frightened out of the frogs and there was no singing that night.

As the days went by, other figures used the log to cross on their journey and carelessly tossed trash into the water below. The pond soon became choked with debris. The water was dirty and dark. It looked as if it were dying.

On a certain afternoon, the sky darkened directly over the pond. Thunder boomed, lightning cracked, and the clouds spilled torrents of rain down into the sad and lifeless pond. It rained and rained and fresh raindrops began to replace the stale water. A lightning bolt struck the log and split it into a thousand pieces.

When the travelers came and saw that their bridge was destroyed, they decided that crossing the pond was no longer the easiest way to go, and they set out in another direction.

The pond was left in peace. Each time it rained, the water became cleaner and more clear. Fish could be seen swimming about, bugs danced, and once more frogs sang their melodies among the flowers and plants.

Just when all seemed reborn, a great noise was heard again. A dark figure approached the pond, and every living thing trembled and held its breath. The figure stopped at the water's edge and looked into the pond. All was still and quiet. Uncertainty hung in the air. At last the figure sat down and, being careful not to disturb any plant or animal, enjoyed the beauty of it all for a very long time.

Journey of the Circle

Diane Ponti

ubilation reigned and the kingdom rejoiced, for it had vanquished its enemies after a long and costly war. The knights had returned home and their swords were put away.

In one corner of the kingdom there lived a young knight and his damsel. The knight was a wild boy and his bride a beautiful maiden. He had found her high in the mountains and lured her from her family's lair. She was young, quiet, and shy, but with a will of iron that matched his wild spirit.

During the long years of war they had lived by the sea while the knight forged the soldiers' swords. When the raucous war ended, and it was time for the things of peace, the knight's wife bore a babe, a girl, whose eyes contained the wildness of the knight and the will of the damsel.

But the knight missed the forging of the mighty swords of war and the damsel missed the freedom she had known by the sea.

The little family had no home. So the damsel and her babe went back to the mountains, to the home of her mother and her sister, while the knight was left behind to build a cottage. Now the new mother felt her freedom had truly flown. She was back to being a maiden again, fettered by her powerful mother and mountaintop ways. Her dashing knight had become distant Father.

The knight, as he built the cottage, resented the loss of his damsel's warm body, the warm body which now belonged to this girl-child. He sought solace with other knights of the kingdom and pretended he was free again. He raged over his fate.

Separation and confusion leaked their poison. The babe was blamed for this venomous spill.

The masks of loneliness and motherhood replaced the damsel's youthful beauty. She waited nine months for her cottage to be built, and during this time she made another creation. It was a tangled web she wove about herself to keep her will safe and strong, a web she wove all night and day. Its thread was fine, the finest gossamer in the land, so fine it was invisible to all. But it was a strong thread. No laughter slipped through its intricate knots and no tears penetrated its solid weave.

The babe watched her mother and her endless weaving. She saw the growing knots and struggled to break through them, tangling herself in their threads. Frustrated by her failure, the babe took comfort in the laps of her grandmother and aunt, but still she missed her mother—her smile, her skin, her touch. The threads and knots were always in the way.

When the cottage was ready and the girl and her mother returned to the knight, the girl-child looked at her mother, cocooned in the safety of her invincible threads, and at her father, trapped in the fury of his voices of rage, and she keened, "I am lost." She knew she was alone. Despair flooded the babe as she lay in the shadows and gazed through the bars of her crib.

Her mother's web of tangled thread had grown mightily as the babe grew bold in her demands. And as the child grew and tried to venture out to see what the world held, the mother panicked in fear. What harm might befall her innocent babe? The mother had the fierceness to protect the child, but her invisible threads pinned her arms and muffled her voice.

The child pushed ahead. She had a flame within her, a flame that threatened the fine threads of her mother's web and that angered her father. It reminded him of his own lost spark, and he worked to rid his daughter of her annoying flame. He allowed no laughter in the cottage. No tears were allowed to spill. No out-of-place noise was permitted.

The damsel and her knight thought that if they could only kill this child's spirit, domestic tranquillity would reign. They sent her to the Elders for help, the Ravens who guarded the gates to Good and Evil and who held the keys of Knowledge.

"Help us, oh powerful Ravens. Teach our babe the ways of girl-children in this world. The foolish child thinks she is a god and acts accordingly. She questions authority, she is rebellious, and her flame still has the power to scorch. Teach her who is boss."

The Ravens went to work. They stared at the

babe with piercing eyes and tight mouths. Their skin, stretched parchment thin, held a gray pall and smelled of cheese. They penetrated the babe's defenses with their eyes. All the sins of her past were laid before her: selfish ingratitude, noisy demands, her annoying flame.

The Ravens shook their heads and scowled. The girl-child felt the crush of their disapproval and could say nothing. She hung her head in shame before their power.

The Ravens' cruel cackles resounded in the wind. Their beady eyes read her soul. "Hah, you are afraid to move. You will die in this spot, pitiful creature. Gone, your Self will be gone. Can you not see it leaving you now? Your uniqueness, your humor, your life. You will lose your Self by denying yourself. You will become nothing. You will be an empty vessel, filled with whatever is haphazardly poured inside. The slop of happenstance will be your drunken guide. Then you will be ready for our world, girl-child."

Stumbling in the wind, the child returned to the cottage. The damsel and her knight were happy. Their fiery little babe, who had caused so much trouble, had been tamed. She had become so much easier to control. The mother could relax her frantic weaving and the father could have a little quiet.

But the girl's spirit was not completely gone. At moments of play, deep in the dark forest, the flame of independence would blaze again and warm her soul.

One night, in a dream, a fiery red ball of smoke

and rattles filled the little girl. A snake slithered from the vapors and curled round and round in the middle of her middle. "Rise, shriveled spirit," commanded the Snake. "I know you are tucked inside this shell of a girl-child. Come and listen to me for a moment."

The girl's spirit stirred within and emerged to listen to the whispers of the Snake. "Be free," the Snake hissed. It whispered with its snake voice in the language only the soul can understand. The girl could hear the sounds, but she could not hear the words. She thought, "Here is the very message of my life, but cotton clouds surround the words and tangle their meanings in a gauzy haze. I strain to hear and all I get are garbled sounds."

The smoke grew thicker, the rattles louder. There was something familiar in the voice of the Snake. It reminded her of the muffled voice of her mother, speaking through her invisible threads. The child relaxed into the sounds of the wise Snake. She quit straining to hear every word, and instead leaned back and let the melody sink into her soul.

Peace descended upon her. She knew then that although her mother's spirit was imprisoned by its web of thread, her voice had escaped and visited her through this Snake. The wisdom of how to defeat the Ravens' prophecy was hissing through the tongue of the Snake that sat curled in the middle of her being.

"You will be saved, my child," hissed the Snake. "Do not doubt the power of your flame. It is strong within you and must be kept alive. Yours will be a lonely journey. Your mother cannot leave her prison of thread. Your father cannot hear you. But I will help you. I will guide you past the Ravens. You will rage against the injustice of this world, and you will be wounded by its power. Your journey must be confusing and demanding so when you are done, you will know where you have been."

The Snake coiled and re-coiled, shook its rattles and continued. "You are going to lose your Self again. In the world of the Ravens, you will be cloaked in your female skin, but you will act as a man and you will then understand his pain. This will be a time of darkness that seems like light, a tunnel of pain that seems a passage of pleasure."

The girl sighed and dreamed on. She understood the Snake's words. It said, "Your greatest danger will be yourself. Your greatest savior will be yourself. The Ravens will tempt you. They will offer prizes of power, prestige, and wealth and dangle baubles before your eyes. When you win their prizes, you will buy their respect. But the price you pay will be your self-respect. In the dark nights when you awaken long before dawn, you will feel the pain in the middle of yourself. You will be perplexed. You will have won all the Ravens' prizes, but the ache will still be there. It will grow with every prize you win.

"You must find your pain. Name it. Claim it for your own. Turn it around. Shake it. Pull it up and out and through you. Let its dust balls and cobwebs and connecting threads billow to the winds. I will visit you in your dreams and waking, but I will be in disguise. It is your task to recognize me when I come. Take my message to heart so you can continue on your journey.

"Yours is not a journey that takes you up through the world or down into the world, but a journey that takes you around the world, so when you are done, you will be where you started. You will have completed the circle. Only then will you be whole again.

"Now go, go into the Ravens' world, girl-child. Win their prizes. Lose your Self. You will find your Self again. You are strong, girl-child. Do not lose your faith or despair of your mistakes.

"Let your mother help you. Do not lose heart at the sight of your mother's cocoon of silence. She speaks to you through me. She protects you through me. She touches you through me. She tells her love of you through me. Look upon her with kindness and forgiveness. She is me. You are her. You are me. The child you will bear is her. We are all one. We have power beyond what the world of men and Ravens possess. It is we who are the Creators. No one else. Remember that, girl-child, on your journey of the circle. We are the Creators."

The Journey to the Ancient Ones

Judi A. Singleton

When I was young, a very old woman told me a story. She told it as a tale from a dream world, but I believe it was more than a dream.

This was her story:

I ran and ran, pursued by an inner urgency that told me I must hurry to reach the Ancient Ones before it was too late.

Why must I go? What was so urgent about my mission? My questions had no answers. I only knew that I must race to get there. I ran across scorched lands where the earth looked like cracked leather, and my feet blistered on the hot surface. The earth sizzled hot in the sun. The blisters on my feet broke, and the skin dried and crumbled like autumn leaves.

Dying people cried hoarsely and reached to me, brushing my ankles. I stopped to give a sip of water to a hag whose skin hung loose on her baked bones. I put a bit of meat into the mouth of a crying child. I stumbled on. When I paused, flashes of pain swirled in front of my eyes. Only my compelling mission to reach the Ancient Ones drove me on.

Before me I saw a dark opening in the earth.

As I approached the cave, a soft coolness surrounded me. My eyes, blind in the dark after the searing, bright light of the sun, adjusted to the darkness and I saw the entrance to a vast pit. I peered into it and saw a ladder, descending into the bowels of nowhere. Quaking with fear, I climbed down the ladder, down and down, pressing on so I could discover the Ancient Ones in time. Deep in the pit, I was enveloped by the quiet and dampness. It soothed me, and my fears faded as I stepped off the ladder onto soft sand.

I lay on the sand, feeling it wear my blistered skin away, and thought that now I would die of thirst. At that moment, I heard water lapping against the shore, and I strained to roll my parched body toward the sound. When I reached it, I fell in and drank my fill. Greedily I drank too much, and vomited, and learned to satisfy my thirst with small sips.

Out of the darkness came a light, bathing me in brightness and illuminating the pit. The walls were sparkling crystal that reflected in the water in a shimmering display. "I've been too long in the heat," I mused. "Or maybe I am dreaming."

I heard a bumping sound and noticed a rubber raft, floating in the water and moored to a reed. I climbed in and set it loose, and the raft drifted away as I lay in the bottom, lulled, serene, with no sense of time. Bobbing like a cork, it floated along the underground river. Suddenly the boat bumped hard against the shore, jarring me from my reverie. I looked up and saw on my right a set of steep stairs rising against the face of a high cliff. I crawled from the raft and began to mount the stairs, feeling my feet on the cold stone and the strain of the muscles in my legs as I climbed.

I could feel the exertion, but when I looked down I saw that I had no body. It had dissolved like a sugar cube in water. I clung to my phantom limbs, yet some magic had stolen the agreement between my body and the atoms that created it.

Where the stairs ended against the cliff was an oak door with a lion's-head knocker. I raised a non-existent hand to touch the door knocker and saw only empty space, but at that moment the door swung silently open, just as if someone had shouted, "Open sesame." I entered a cave. A fire shed light, so I could see the entire cavern. The hearth was large enough for a grown man to stand upright and again as wide. The fire crackled and snapped, sending the pungent smell of cedar throughout the cave. How could I sense these things when I had no eyes to see or nose to smell? I glided forward to a rocking chair by the fire, and I sensed a presence and I knew it was one of the Ancient Ones. Cowled and hooded, swathed in black, she mingled with the shadows.

I sat in the rocker, transfixed and wondering, as she transformed into a baby, then to a young woman, then to a hag. I knew then that this was a holy chamber and the home of the Ancient Ones, and I felt I had been here before. I was not afraid, but the Ancient One's changing shapes filled me with a yearning, and I moved to her and put my head (but I had no head) in the Ancient One's lap. She stroked my hair (but I had no hair) and crooned as one does to a child. I felt myself transforming, changing shapes, and I said, loudly, "So, Mother, you are me and I created all, all of this. I have accomplished my mission."

The shadows shifted and the flame blazed white and quickly was extinguished into blackness.

The Moth and the Butterfly

Andrea Scott Abernethy

n a time that now seems long ago, a winged creature flew through an open window into a child's bedroom. The child watched in amazement as the creature fluttered, then fell to the ground. The child reached out a hand, and the creature staggered to it awkwardly and climbed onto one finger.

The drab creature had no color except for two black dots at the tips of its wings. It seemed to the child that it too was very fragile and alone.

The child stared closely and then asked the creature, "Who are you, and why have you come?"

The creature replied. "You ask who I am and I can only say I truly don't know. My destiny is to be a butterfly, but as you can see, I am a moth. It would take a miracle to change from a moth to a butterfly, yet somehow I feel that is what I was destined to be. I sense that you too have a purpose in life that is different from the way you are now. Perhaps our fates are entwined and our meeting will help us both."

The child fetched a jar from the shelf and said to the moth, "I will make this your home." The moth fluttered its wings and agreed, and the child placed the moth into the jar. The others in the household laughed and chided the child, and said it was foolish to keep a moth. But the child set the jar on a table and brought leaves for the moth to eat, and the child and the moth became friends.

The two friends talked when no one else was around. They talked of their loneliness, and how different they felt from those around them. The child asked if the moth was a boy or a girl. The moth replied that it did not know; color and grace were its only way of knowing. The child said, "That is my way, too." All that the moth was sure of was that some day it would become what it was meant to be, a glorious butterfly. The child never doubted that this was true.

Months passed. Patiently the child watched the jar and continued to add fresh foliage to it. Nothing happened. There was no change. Then, one morning, in through the window flew a huge butterfly with dazzling golden wings. It perched on the edge of the jar and fluttered weakly. "I need water," it whispered. "And I need nectar from the honeysuckle."

The child hurried to bring water. The moth offered blossoms from the honeysuckle vine in its jar. The butterfly sipped and rested, and when it was revived it said, "You have been kind to me. In return, I will grant you a wish, for I am a butterfly with magic powers."

"I have only one wish," the moth said. "I want to be a butterfly just like you. I have wanted that all my life, I am not happy as a moth."

"That is my wish too," said the child. "I want to see the moth become a butterfly."

The butterfly said, "You are asking for something very difficult, but if that is your wish you shall have it. It won't be easy. You will have to give up your familiar life as a moth. You will have to be a larva, a caterpillar, a chrysalis, a cocoon before you can be a butterfly. Are you willing to go through all that?"

The moth trembled with excitement. "Yes, yes, of course!"

The butterfly said, "Then it is done." And it flew away.

The child and the moth talked into the night about what the butterfly had said, and finally fell into weary sleep.

In the morning the child rushed to the jar. There the moth perched on a leaf, looking just as it had the day before. There was no change. Had the butterfly been only a dream?

The weeks went by. Summer turned to fall and fall to winter, and still the child brought food to the jar. The natural world was now dark, gray, and cold. The rains came and with them shorter days. A chill swallowed the land. The child and the moth began to give up hope.

But one day a change came. The child looked into the jar, and there, curled among the leaves at the bottom, was a caterpillar. The moth was nowhere to be seen. The child spoke to the caterpillar. It did not move or answer, and the child thought it must be dead. The great and magical change had not worked. The butterfly was wrong.

Anger and a great feeling of loss welled up in

the child, and tears of abandonment and rejection poured forth. Then a tiny, weak voice spoke. The child blinked away the tears and looked closely at the jar. There was the caterpillar, crawling slowly up the vine. It brushed the child's finger with its fuzzy body and said, "I am small and weak, but the miracle is happening. Please keep me near, and have faith."

As winter turned to spring and spring to early summer, the child put honeysuckle vines in the jar. Gradually, the caterpillar's size and color changed, and the creature knew its time had come. In the wee hours of the summer night, it crawled up the honeysuckle vine one last time.

It attached itself to the top of the stem and began to spin, choosing this place so the child could watch. As the morning sun rose and flooded the room, there was a metamorphosis in the making. The caterpillar was gone, and all the child could see was something small, compact and still.

As it had begun in the wee hours of the rising sun, so too it would be again. Now in the rising of the second moon the cocoon began to move. The child watched and waited and put fresh honeysuckle, damp with morning dew, into the jar. The morning waned, the sun rose higher in the sky. The moment of new life had arrived. Slowly the cocoon twisted and turned, until it burst apart.

The moment came. The child's eyes were as big as saucers. Tears fell. The dream and the wish had come true. A magnificent butterfly rose to the rim of the jar, sat still, and slowly spread her wings to the fully extended position.

The child and the butterfly sat and stared at each other.

They said, "We have given each other life. Now it is time that we merge and set ourselves free."

The child held the butterfly on one hand and walked to the wide open window and set her gently on the windowsill. The child crawled onto her back, and under a summer sun they rose united on butterfly wings and flew triumphantly into the day.

The Red Ball

Pamela Penney

nce upon a time, there lived a mother and six daughters. The youngest daughter, Jane, was always made to cook and clean and wait on her mother and sisters, simply because she was the youngest. The mother and the other daughters bossed Jane day in and day out. They gave her hand-me-down rags to wear and let her eat only their leftover scraps of food.

The youngest child had no time to think or do for herself because the others in the home always made such messes and then threw fits, demanding that she come to clean up after them. The mother and older daughters ate a lot, too, so the youngest was either cooking or washing up, when she wasn't running here and there to keep them happy.

One morning, as Jane was collecting firewood, she found a bright red ball hidden behind a thorny bush. She pulled it out, brushed off the thorns, and began to bounce and play with it. She had such fun with the new ball that she almost forgot to collect the firewood. Suddenly remembering, she put the beautiful red ball into her pocket and resumed her chore, working quickly so she would not be missed by the others.

The next morning, as the youngest daughter

put on her worn dress, which had belonged to four sisters before her, she thought about the red ball and hurried to get outside to play with it. This time as she bounced the ball, she heard someone say, "Ouch!" and then, "Hey! Not so hard!" Jane stopped bouncing the ball and heard the same voice say, "Thank you." The child stuck the ball into her pocket and dashed behind a tree, thinking someone was watching her playing instead of collecting firewood, as she had been told. She felt something wriggling about in her pocket. She reached in and pulled out the red ball.

"Oh! You startled me!" said the child to the ball.

"I had to get you to stop bouncing me so hard," replied the ball.

"How are you able to speak?" asked the child.

"I used to be a young woman," began the ball. "I had older sisters and a mother who had me wait on them hand and foot. I was working so hard to please them that I never learned to take care of myself. I ran around in circles day and night for others, and eventually I ran myself into this red ball. I have been a ball ever since, rolling the countryside, trying to break free and become a person again. When you found me, I had rolled right into that thorn bush."

"Oh, how terrible," said the child. "I will keep you safe in my pocket until we know what to do."

Every morning young Jane played with the ball before collecting the firewood. Taking the time to enjoy herself and play, she was happier than she had ever been. Luckily, the other six were late sleepers and she was never missed that early in the morning. But she had no time to think about ways of setting the ball free from its spell to become a young woman again, because she was constantly busy, running to take care of the household and her mother and older sisters. She ran in so many circles, she began to grow dizzy. After a time the beautiful red ball noticed that when Jane threw her up into the air, her aim wasn't as straight as it had once been.

One morning the girl, now almost a young woman herself, took the ball from her pocket, but she didn't bounce or toss it. "What's the matter?" the ball asked, and Jane answered, "I am so dizzy. I run around and around in circles, working for my family. I have no time to look after myself. If I keep at this pace, I fear that I shall turn into a ball like you."

With that, the red ball began to quiver and shake and roll. It grew larger and larger. Odd shapes began stretching and pushing out of the roundness. The ball rolled and pushed and stretched until, with a puff of red smoke, a beautiful young woman stood where the ball had been. The woman stared at the girl and the girl stared at the young woman in amazement. They looked exactly alike. "I'm confused," Jane said. "You look just like me."

The young woman explained that she had come to help Jane see her predicament with her family. The woman was the child and the child was the woman, they were one and the same. The young woman had come in the form of the ball to teach the child how to play, to find time for herself away from the others. If Jane had kept going at that pace for her mother and sisters, she surely would have turned into a ball—beautiful but good only to be used by someone else.

Then Jane understood. She was happy to realize that she didn't have to wait on anyone but herself anymore. Jane went to embrace the young woman, but with a puff of smoke the woman was gone, for she and the child truly were one and the same.

The youngest daughter went quickly back to the house of her mother and five sisters, who were still asleep in bed.

"Wake up! Wake up! *You* have firewood to collect and the kettle to put on and mending to tend to!" she declared. The mother and sisters stirred slowly and blinked. "What? What did you say? Get our morning tea!" they demanded.

"No! You get up and fix your own tea! I am not getting your morning tea or your afternoon tea or any other tea. You all are going to have to begin to take care of yourselves because that is exactly what I am going to do— take care of myself." And with that, the young woman began her day, the first of many days of freedom.

Sister She-Mouse

Beverly Thompson

Once upon a time, there was a small she-mouse. She was a furry, cute little mouse who lived in a cozy nest in a hole in the meadow. She was happy to run and play, chasing her shadow and bounding through the grass with the other mice. She liked to feel the sun warm her whiskers. She loved to feel the wind ruffle her fur. She delighted in the raindrops on her little back. Sometimes, however, when she was scurrying around the meadow, she sensed a dark shadow following her, and she would shudder to see a hawk flying above, searching for a meal. She would run, terrified, back into her hole in the ground, looking for her mother to protect her. Her mother was never there. But her sister mice were, comforting her, holding her, and telling her she was safe. She always felt safe and secure and cared for when she could sleep curled in the arms of a sister mouse.

And so She-Mouse grew up.

One day she felt an urge to go beyond the meadow, to explore the world on the other side, the world of trees and shadows and other animals. She knew it was a dangerous venture, into a place full of predators, but she felt drawn to excitement and danger. Somehow she felt more alive when the wind and rain beat down upon her soft brown fur, or when she encountered strange, scary animals.

Somehow she felt more alive when she was running away from dark, shadowy forms.

Somehow she felt more alive when she was pushing beyond her comfortable place as a little mouse in the meadow.

Cautiously she entered the forest, testing the path, smelling for strange creatures. She was certain she did not want to be with animals just like her. Oh, no! She wanted to find a partner who was strong and beautiful, who ran through the wilds unafraid, who ventured into places where She-Mouse had never gone, and who would care for her and protect her from other predators.

She-Mouse got her wish. She met a creature who was not at all like her. He was a fox—large, strong, clever, and very sure of himself. He persuaded her to leave her home and her kind, and to live her life in the forest and the land of the foxes.

The forest was full of darkness and rippling light. At first it was exciting, because it was so very different from the life she had known in the meadow. But after awhile, the differences made her uncomfortable. In the strangeness of the forest, she felt alone and lonely. The mouse began to grow smaller. She became smaller and smaller, until finally she was just a tiny she-mouse again. She-Mouse was often afraid, but she pushed away her fear and hoped that someday she would find the light and joy of the meadow again.

The years sped by. She-Mouse continued to yearn for the warmth and love of home and the feel of her sisters' arms around her. She longed for that strong sense of who she was that she had lost. One day She-Mouse ran away. She ran far from the forest to a strange land. She thought this was a magnificent world. But it was a strange one, with all kinds of unfamiliar creatures, some of them frightening. This world had very few patches of green or fields of weeds and grasses. She-Mouse still missed the meadow.

In that land, she met a few animals who seemed somewhat familiar. She was delighted to mingle with them. She felt a connection that stirred something very deep, something unnamable within her. Yet a restlessness drove her to continue her journey, always searching for the unnamable place. It was not the meadow, but it was … somewhere.

More years flew by. One day on her wanderings, She-Mouse found herself back in the forest and the land of the foxes, and there she met again the creature who had been her companion for so long. Overcome with joy, she returned to her former way of life. She grew bigger, healthier, fatter. Her fur was sleek and long. This life felt good and seemed to fit her. Yet once again, unhappiness began creeping into her days and nights. She started to lose her shine and her glow, and again she became smaller and smaller. Some days she could hardly leave her soft little burrow to go out and look for food.

One day she had a dream. In the dream she

saw herself with a new sister friend, creeping up a huge cliff that overlooked a vast plain with mountains in the distance. Together they viewed the scene as if they were eagles. Behind them lay the dark, crowded, sinister forest. She-Mouse began to play with her new sister friend— happy, contented play, adventurous play. Their silly, lazy play went on for hours, taking She-Mouse into places she had never known. This made the world that She-Mouse lived in seem even more wrong for her, and now, in her dream, she realized that she could not return to the land of the foxes. In that instant, she also knew she no longer belonged exclusively to the world of the mice. Something was happening to her that seemed out of her control and very frightening.

After this dream She-Mouse felt troubled, lost, and lonely, and she dived deep into her mouse hole and pondered and wept. She fell asleep, and when she wakened, she found herself curled up in the arms of the sister-friend of her dream. She was half-mouse and half-fox.

"I have found you," She-Mouse said.

"No," said her sister, "you have found *you*."

The Sacred Gifts
Debra Clement

nce upon a time, many seasons ago, a child-to-be was called forth by the Great Spirit. The Spirit said, "Little one, the time has come for your life on Earth. Many lessons and gifts are waiting there for you. You will grow in your Earth-mother's womb, and become a baby girl, and be named Debra. While you are tucked away in the womb, the Grandmother of your people will visit you. She will teach you what you need to know before you begin your own journey on Earth."

And so the child's Earth life began. Just as the Great Spirit had told her, she nestled in a womb that fed her and sustained her. But the Earth mother who carried her also taught her that the world to come was a place of danger and distrust. Night and day, her Earth mother whispered, blood to blood, of suffering. Debra learned that she would be born into a body she could not be proud of, a body that would shame her and cause her pain.

When the child-to-be heard these predictions, she was afraid. She wondered if it might be better not to be born at all. She was enjoying herself, dreamily floating in this protected place; she liked the way the warm liquid felt on her skin. She was content to languish in the warmth of the sacred space, feeling her earth-body form. What would it be like not having these pleasurable sensations any more? What kind of fearful world was this going to be, where she would feel shame and misery? And then she had a new feeling: she felt powerless. It was too late, she had no choice. Like it or not, she was going to be born into this strange world.

The months passed in dark solitude, and the girl-to-be absorbed her Earth mother's sadness and pain before she herself had seen one streak of sunlight.

On the day before her birth, Grandmother arrived, a wrinkled old woman wrapped in robes of wisdom. Quietly she said to Debra, "I carry ancient secrets, the wisdom of the women who have come before you. I bring you two gifts. One is for protection, the other for power."

The first was a song of healing, Debra's own song that would comfort and protect her, and be a source of strength for the life to come. Grandmother placed it gently in the almost-born infant's mouth, under her tongue, and the soothing notes were absorbed into her spirit.

The second gift was a dream dance, a celebration of womanhood and creativity, given to be Debra's power. Grandmother enveloped the child in a blanket of gold, and through each pore and cell the dance was absorbed into her spirit.

When she had given her gifts, Grandmother prepared to leave. She said, "Remember, you travel this journey for a reason, to play out your dream. Never forget to sing your song and dance your dance. This is all you need to find your joy. I must leave you now, but I will always be with you." And with that, she was gone like the melting mist.

"I felt something strange just now," Debra's Earth mother said. "As if there were a third presence in my body. And then it was gone."

Earth mother had never whispered to Debra of joy or power. What did these new words mean? The infant, on this last day before she was born, wondered if she could believe them. But they had entered her being, and she forgot her mother's whispers and the predictions of gloom, the promises of trouble. On her day of birth she emerged with hope. Within her was a golden light that created a soft warmth in her belly. She had her dream dance to perform, and the music of her healing song resonated in her soul. She felt joy, because the Grandmother spirit was with her. And when she looked upon the abundant Earth and the flaming sun and fertile soil, she decided her mother was mistaken. How could harm come to her in this beautiful place?

But the time of safety was short. Soon, in a moment created from her mother's worst imaginings, Earth's beauty was violently transformed. Angry clouds darkened the sky, and the ground rumbled in rage. The earth split open, and a flood of demons was released. The demons entered the bodies of men in Debra's world, and their red eyes glowed with the pleasure of destruction. They spoke words of magic to the women in Debra's world, and they turned the women's hearts to stone.

The child sought frantically for refuge. To make

herself silent and safe, she swallowed her healing song. To make herself invisible, she froze the dream dance. But her body betrayed her presence, and she could not escape.

> A glowing red gaze
> outstretched hands
> a blanket of black
> sleep.

When she arose, head bowed in shame, she put on a mourning cloak made of a thousand tears and remembered nothing.

As Debra's childhood days passed, she felt lonely and lost, longing for a home she could not recall. The familiar faces in her world were merely masks. She forgot the song of healing and the dream dance. She did not remember a time when her body was a pleasant dwelling place. She found no solace in her Earth mother, whose dreams had died long ago.

Empty of spirit, Debra filled her body with food, creating a thick protective shell to deaden her pain and cover her sorrow.

Empty of spirit, Debra filled her mind with facts and sought satisfaction in a quest for perfection.

When she became an adult, she traveled to distant lands, always searching for a home, looking for it in the eyes of strangers. Sometimes she would meet a glowing red gaze that made her body tremble in recognition and fear. She searched as one who has lost a dear friend. Many times she thought she'd found one, but always she would waken and find herself alone.

For many years she wandered, until she became weary with travel and weak in faith. One day, exhausted, she fell asleep in a quiet place under a tree. She dreamed of the days of danger, and as she wakened, emerging from the silence came the faint sounds of a comforting melody. Debra did not know it, but the golden light that flickered within her was leading her home.

Slowly she began to remember the time before the danger and shame. With each memory the golden light grew brighter, and she closed her eyes and followed it to its source. She grew nearer, and the light became a blazing fire that illuminated a shadowy cave. Hovering over the flame was a familiar figure. "Grandmother," Debra said. The old woman turned and opened her arms.

Grandmother led Debra into the cave. From deep within the earthen floor she pulled the song of healing and the dream dance and presented them to her granddaughter for the second time.

"I've kept these for you all these years," she said. "Now it is time for you to use them, to find your joy."

Debra wept for all the lost years, and Grandmother said, "Those years were not wasted, my dear. Your journey has taught you the meaning of your gifts, and your pain has made them sacred."

Debra nodded. No longer a child, she understood. She took off her mourning cloak made of tears and tossed it upon the fire. It sizzled and burned, and as the flames grew higher, she threw back her head and laughed.

It was time to sing her song and dance her dance. She was home.

The Tree Necklace

Mickey Barnett

The Spirit of Creation was an enormous cube, slick and shiny as stainless steel, and as it traveled through the universe, it came across a newly formed planet. There was no life on this planet except for one thing, The Tree.

The Spirit thought it would be entertaining to create a life form and supply it with everything it needed. And with the thought, The Man appeared.

Then the Creation Spirit created cubes and hung them high in The Tree. The Spirit said to The Man, "Everything you will need is contained in these cubes. Each will fall to the ground and open as it is needed, each one in its own time."

Another spirit in the cosmos, Nature, had been silently watching. Nature had seen much of Beauty, Power, Hope, and Love in her travels through the universe and longed to share them with The Man. She knew that he could appreciate them and care for them as she did. So she rolled the essence of each into a shiny, colored sphere and strung the spheres together and placed them at the top of The Tree. There they swayed and glittered while The Man watched from below. The Man was in awe of Nature's necklace, and The Tree became an object of devotion and reverence.

As time passed, The Man grew greedy, and filled the planet with factories, pollution, and waste. The Spirit of Creation sighed and moved on.

The Man became discontented. The cubes were falling too slowly from The Tree, and he coveted Nature's shiny necklace. He took an axe and he cut down The Tree, and as it fell the necklace broke. The spheres rolled around the world, each one coming to rest in a deep crevasse, where it disappeared from sight.

Nature saw The Tree fall. She saw the necklace break and the spheres roll away, and she grieved. Tears rolled down her cheeks as she wept and wept. She cried so many tears that lakes and rivers and oceans formed on the planet. When she saw all this water she smiled, and as she smiled, the spheres of the broken necklace cracked open, and new life emerged. Green plants and trees, colorful fruits and flowers, animals and insects and birds and music came forth. Where The Tree had stood, a woman appeared, wearing a necklace of brightly colored beads.

Nature said to the Tree Woman, "You are one with this planet, and you are its guardian. You are the past, the present, and the future. In you is all that you will need."

Star Child

Jeanette Chardon

nce upon a time, a girl-child was born. As she lay in her crib, a star came into her room and settled on her chest. The star began to pulsate in harmony with the child's breathing, until the star entered into her and they became one. The star child was bright, adventurous, and fun-loving. She had quick wit and a musical laugh. She often sang and danced. She loved movement and music. She loved exploring and playing out-of-doors. When she was very small, she had no family, so she was free to roam and discover. She enjoyed her life, for there was little restriction and she was always provided for.

Then the star child came to the attention of the Powers That Be, and they decided she needed more structure. She was taken in by a family. At first, she liked being with this family. As she grew older, however, the male members of the family began to take advantage of her. She accepted this as a part of the great adventure, but soon it became a heavy burden. It was clear that the males in the family were not interested in her enjoyment; they were interested in using her only for their own pleasure. She became miserable. Her star wanted to drift away and leave her, so she held it fast and hid it away in a secret chamber within where it would be safe. With her star hidden, her light began to dim. Her music became sour and discordant. She no longer danced. She seldom went out-doors. In fact, she seldom moved at all, except to attend to life's most basic necessities.

One night, as the star child lay sleeping, a black cat entered her room. It leapt upon her bed and sniffed her mouth and nose. It purred loudly and lay upon her chest. The girl and the cat began to breathe in unison, until the cat entered into her and they became one.

The next day, the girl moved differently. Her movements were no longer the graceful dance-move-ments of the star child. Nor were they the stiff movements of the girl who was used. They were stealthy, stalking, cat-like movements. The girl howled, and she yowled. When she opened her mouth, people would cover their ears. Now when the male members of the family came to her, she would yowl and she would claw and bite. And then she would be left alone. Quietly, like a satisfied cat, she would smile.

One night, the cat girl's foster father came into her room. She heard him coming, and the hackles on her neck rose. She was poised to claw, to yowl. But this night, her foster father came bearing a whip. He came to scare the cat out of the girl. He came to beat the cat out of the girl. And he tried. When he finished, her back was cov-ered with the welts of his lashes. Her arms were covered with the welts of his lashes. Even her face had angry red welts across it.

The cat girl cried. The cat wanted to escape,

but the girl held her tightly. She locked the cat in a chamber deep within where she would be safe.

That night, as she lay sleeping, a weasel crept into her room. It leapt upon her bed and sniffed around her mouth and nose. It lay down upon her chest and began to breathe in unison with her until it entered into her and they became one.

The next day, the young woman moved differently. Her movements were not the graceful dance-movements of the star child, nor were they the stiff movements of the girl who was used. Nor were they the stalking, stealthy movements of the cat girl. These were the purposeful movements of one who knows where she is going and who knows the shortest route to get there. Before there were stirrings in the other rooms of the house, the weasel girl was up. She packed a few necessities and a little money, and she was gone. She went straight to the highway and accepted rides headed to the place where she wanted to go. She traveled five hundred miles, a thousand miles. On the way, she learned a lot. She learned how to get what she needed. She learned how to survive.

During her young adulthood she found other weasel people who were clinging tenaciously to survival just as she was. She used them to survive. They used her to survive. She met a weasel man, and the two of them thought they could survive better together. They married, and weasel woman was blessed with four children: Sacrifice, Love, Patience, and Joy. As each was born, she became even more tenacious about surviving and protecting her little ones.

One night, as she lay sleeping, she heard a strange noise. It was the most beautiful sound she had ever heard, like glorious music, and it came from some deep cavernous place within herself. She began to listen.

When she woke, the woman was different. Her movements were those of the weasel woman, but once in a while she would stop and look at some far-off place and hear a far-off voice. At times she would hum or sing a shred of a song. She tried to tell her weasel husband about her experience, but it made him feel strange and uncomfortable. He would not stop clinging to survival long enough to listen to some wild chant. And so, for years, she listened and occasionally sang pieces of songs that came from a memory of a long-ago place and time.

One night, as she lay sleeping, she heard a strange noise. It was the most moving and exotic noise she had ever heard, like howling, and it came from some deep, cavernous place within herself. Intrigued, she began to listen.

When she woke, the woman was different. She was still the weasel woman, clinging tenaciously to survival, but every once in a while she moved with grace and stealth, quietly and covertly. She also began to grow brighter and lighter. She would occasionally laugh and joke and burst out singing. Her four children loved seeing the changes in their mother, but her weasel husband scoffed at her frivolity. He was intent upon clinging tenaciously to survival. Often she would pick up her four children and carry them away to wander in a star-glimmering land, but her weasel husband would not come.

One night, while she lay sleeping, the singing and the yowling became louder. She could no longer deny the source of these sounds. She flung open the dusty lids of the chambers where her star and her cat had been hidden away for so long, and she embraced them both as long-lost friends. As the three were savoring their reunion, an eagle flew in through the window and alighted upon her chest. The eagle beat her wings in unison with the woman's breathing and the cat's purring and the star's glimmering until the eagle entered into the woman and they became one. And as she lay sleeping, the eagle, the weasel, the cat, and the star decided that it was time to move on, to discover what life was like when one was not merely clinging tenaciously to survival.

When she woke, the woman was different. She was no longer weasel woman, tenacious clinger. She was no longer cat girl, angry yowler. She was no longer star child, fanciful dancer. She was none of these. And she was all of these. She was all of these and she was eagle woman, far-seeing flyer. She was on her way to becoming. She bade her grim weasel husband good-bye, picked up her children, and they went forth together on the road to becoming. They had adventures, they danced, they sang, they laughed, they yowled, and they flew, happily ever after.

The Waters of Deception

Kayci Cavenah

Long ago and far away—just yesterday—there was a young woman named Calibrand. She married a nice man and in due time they had a daughter. The daughter, named Dalisinore, was the apple of her mother's eye. Calibrand tried hard to be a good mother, providing everything she thought her beautiful young daughter needed. Naturally, she protected her from anything that might be harmful, dangerous, or evil.

Near this happy family's little cottage was an enormous lake that was completely surrounded by a high, wide rock wall. The rock wall had been built many years before by the good people of the village to keep their children away from the deep and dangerous lake, named the Waters of Deception. Anyone who fell in came out blind. Wanting only to protect their children, the villagers forbade them to play on or near the wall. It was best to ignore its existence and stay clear of it.

Some children obeyed their parents and never went near the wall and the water. But many of them, like children everywhere, were heedless of the grownups' warnings. Despite all their parents' advice, most of the village children at some point climbed the wall to look down into the Waters of Deception, and eventually they fell in.

Those who came out found themselves stricken blind and unable to find their way home. Their parents were stricken with grief and mourned the loss of their children or became angry and resentful that all their efforts to keep them safe had failed.

Now, Calibrand had loved and nurtured Dalisinore and kept her safe from all of life's problems, including the dreaded waters. Dalisinore adored her mother in return, but as she became older she naturally became more independent. She very much wanted to be a good daughter and please her mother, but she felt a strong need to experience life to the fullest. Unbeknownst to her, some experiences require great amounts of risk and danger. Being the naive child that she was, "risk and danger" looked like "excitement and fun."

So each day as she played with her friends, she came closer and closer to the great rock wall. Eventually, when she became really, really brave, she climbed up and walked upon its upper edge. It was pitifully easy and not nearly as dangerous as everyone had said. It did not seem as if there was any possibility of falling at all. "Aren't those grownups ridiculously silly? And paranoid too!" she thought.

Each day she climbed upon the rock wall and walked further and further. One day she slipped and fell. Over and over she tumbled down the hill, headed straight for the Waters of Deception. Into the dark lake she went, and the waters closed over her head.

Since the water had always been forbidden,

she had never learned to swim. Luckily, though, Dalisinore had a guardian angel who stopped her from going into the deepest part of the lake and certain death. Instead, she came up sputtering in shallow water. Thankfully, believing that everything would be all right as soon as she could wade out of the water, she stood. But when she opened her eyes, she saw nothing but a deep and terrifying darkness. How would she find her way home?

Cold, alone, and afraid, unaware that her guardian angel was guiding her, Dalisinore felt her way back to the rock wall. She didn't know that the Waters of Deception had changed her sight and her vision, and she was doomed to wander the great, wide world alone and in total darkness. When she reached the steep rock wall, she climbed it slowly, feeling for handholds and footholds in the sharp stones, back to the top. She thought she was near the place where she had fallen in. In reality, she was on the other side of the large body of water, far from her home.

Dalisinore came down from the wall and made her way in the world. She found a job to support herself, relying on the simple values that her mother had taught her: honesty and loyalty, truthfulness and hard work. Since she couldn't see, she sharpened her other senses and her intuition.

Dalisinore met a nice young man named Ryanica. She had no idea what he saw in her, but she liked the way she felt around him—warm and safe and peaceful. They fell in love. Over time, Ryanica taught her many things. Most important, he taught her to see without eyes and encouraged her to trust her developing intuition and feel her way.

What he didn't tell her was that he knew a remedy for her condition. He had found it because long ago he too had fallen into the Waters of Deception, and when he came out he sought a cure. He had learned that the blindness was curable for those willing to follow a certain path and learn certain lessons. And he could lead Dalisinore to her cure. So he loved her and watched over her and coaxed her toward her redemption. He set an example by which she could live. He picked her up when she fell down. He encouraged her when she made mistakes. He forgave her when she rebelled. He supported her when she was weak.

As painful as it was for both of them, Ryanica made Dalisinore return and walk the rock wall around the Waters of Deception, in spite of her fear and her anguish and her blindness. When she could walk the entire length of the wall, her feet would tell her when she arrived home. And he would follow her to the ends of the earth until her greater sight, involving all her senses, relieved her blindness.

Dalisinore and Ryanica were married and had two daughters. Of the two daughters, one was very responsible and obedient and one was wild and independent. Not wanting to hinder their growth, Dalisinore put her fears for them aside and began to truly believe that their guardian angels would take care of them just as she had been taken care of. She learned to trust in their ability to make their own way in the world, no matter what evil should befall them, just as she had done. This was part of the lesson she had to learn.

Dalisinore was happy, but still she struggled with her fears. By now she had spent many years walking the rock wall and one day, as she was trudging along, she stopped at a place that felt familiar. It seemed very like her first encounter with the wall. Disbelieving, she called out loud for her mother, and as the words left her lips, a faint light entered her eyes. With newly sensitive ears, she heard the sound of her mother's voice, rejoicing that Dalisinore, her long-lost daughter, had returned.

Calibrand and Dalisinore, mother and daughter, laughed and danced and hugged and cried. Dalisinore was greatly distressed that she had caused her mother so much pain through her childish innocence and ignorance. As each tear dropped, her eyes stung with the bitterness of the long years of separation. Yet with each falling tear, the light in her eyes increased, and her sight became more and more clear, until the world sparkled with crystal reflections.

Not only was Dalisinore blessed by the return of her eyesight, she had learned over the years to use her intuition as well, to produce a clearer and more precise vision. Dalisinore returned for Ryanica and her daughters and brought them home to Calibrand. They all rejoiced and lived happily ever after.

The Beginning

Mickey Barnett

ajera and Pello are twin sisters. Their mother is Wella, the Goddess of Emotion, and their father is Tharius, God of Intellect. Pajera and Pello have reached the age of the acquisition of power and they are anxious to begin practice.

There is no evil or malice in Pajera or Pello. They are, however, young goddesses full of spirit and curiosity. Pajera is the godly embodiment of the question why and Pello the question how. Together, as they grow older, they will become the Goddesses of Truth and Beauty.

Wella, having raised other children, is aware that the practice of power is at first unruly and undisciplined and sometimes destructive. So she takes her children to a far corner of the Milky Way, to a barren planet that has previously been used as a training ground for young gods and goddesses. The planet is lifeless, flat, and gray as far as the eye can see. With a final hug and farewell and a caution to be careful, Wella leaves her daughters for their week of initiation.

Pajera and Pello immediately vie to see who has the greater power. Pajera calls on the clouds to flood the planet, while Pello moves the sun closer to dry up the rain in great gusts of steam. Pajera throws meteors at the planet below, creating vast craters, while Pello crashes the clouds together to make rolling thunder. Pajera moves huge amounts of soil that become towering mountains, and Pello collects moisture that forms immense bodies of water. Pajera moves the stars closer to brighten the night skies, while Pello spins the planet on an invisible axis.

Eventually Pajera and Pello tire of their power contest and play a game of lightning tag. Chasing each other with bolts of lightning, they roam the planet, hiding behind mountains and beneath oceans, rising above the clouds, and burying themselves under the soil. As they are about to stop for a rest, one last lightning bolt cracks from Pello's hand. It strikes a small, muddy pond. While Pajera and Pello rest and renew their powers, the atoms and molecules in the pond are excited by the lightning's electrical charge and congregate together to form living units.

These tiny units begin to divide. Quickly, for time to the gods, even small ones, is measured much differently from ours, they develop the capacity to breathe and think and move and feel.

Pello awakens to see these small creatures huddled together in the shade of a mountain. She nudges Pajera, who rises with a start. "Why are they here? What are they?" Pajera asks, staring at the creatures.

"I'm not sure," answers Pello. "What I'd like to know is how they got here."

Pajera reaches down to examine one of the creatures, accidentally crushing it. She throws it aside and carefully picks up another. But the creature is so small and fragile, she injures it just by handling it. Pello snatches it from her sister's hand. "How does it work?" she asks, turning the creature over and upside down. Pello holds it by the neck to examine the body, and it stops moving.

"What are you doing?" booms a voice from far above the sisters' heads. It is the combined voices of the girls' parents, coming to take them home.

Wella swoops down, landing beside her daughters. "Oh my," she says with a sigh, "these are living beings! They must not be abused and killed. You girls have never seen life such as this before, you knew no better. You must respect these creatures and care about them. How do you think they feel, being so small and helpless?"

"What can we do for them?" the girls ask.

"I'll put some thought into that," Tharius says. "I've read about creatures like these, and I know a great deal about them. I understand some things about them and what they need."

"And I'll examine the feelings I sense from them," Wella cries. "That should help us to understand what they want."

"For heaven's sake!" adds a new voice. "Thinking and examining and feeling won't get anything accomplished!" This is Cerdis, the girls' grandmother, the Goddess of Wisdom and Compassion. "Let's ask the creatures what they want and need and give it to them!"

The small creatures line up two by two, awed and respectful and excited. Cerdis asks each pair to tell her their desires.

The first ones want to be tall and live long lives. They become the forests.

The second pair wish to live in the oceans and become fish.

The third pair say they want to roam the planet and live off the land. They become the beasts.

The fourth pair want to lift free from the earth. They are the birds.

The fifth set of creatures wishes to live close to the soil and bring beauty and health to the planet. These become the plants and flowers and grains.

The sixth and final set of creatures remains silent for a time. Finally they say in unison, "We want to stay as we are. The planet is beautiful and contains all that we need. Our wish is to have all the colors of the rainbow represented on earth and the sounds that the young goddesses make when they sing. With these our world will be complete."

The creatures' wishes are fulfilled and the family of gods and goddesses leaves to return home. Grandmother Cerdis smiles, and all is good in the universe.

In the Realm of Rituals

Angela

nce upon a time in a far-off forest, there lived a princess named Andreena. The forest was evil. It remained dark even on the brightest of sunny days. Andreena was afraid of this forest, called the Realm of Rituals, which held many secrets.

In the Realm of Rituals were ancient oak trees that had lived for centuries and saw all that went on in the forest. Andreena was afraid of the oak trees, especially at night. Evil spirits roamed the Realm of Rituals during the day and settled into the oak trees at night.

The oak trees loomed above all else, and their branches kept the forest hidden. The trunks of these oaks were gnarled and scarred. The oaks were known to grab little children who tried to run away and hold them until the guards came to claim them. The guards shared secrets with the oaks.

Also in the Realm of Rituals was the Mystical Swamp. The Mystical Swamp held the souls of the dead who could not escape. Snakes kept inventory of the swamp dwellers. The snakes were as dark as the depths of the Mystical Swamp. Andreena knew all about the Mystical Swamp and stayed as far away as she could from it.

Many animals inhabited the Realm of Rituals.

There were white-tailed deer, peaceful, gentle creatures. Andreena loved to watch them with their fawns as they nibbled the fresh green grass at the edge of the forest. But Andreena had to be careful. When she was not looking, the white-tails would change. The evil spirits in the forest would sense her peace and inhabit one of the white-tails. Then the gentle white-tail would become as evil as the spirit that had taken over her presence. Her soft brown eyes became glowing red, her silky fur became matted, and a snarl on her mouth revealed angry fangs.

This creature would stalk Andreena until she knew it was there, and in that instant pounce on her. Andreena felt horrible pain as this creature ripped into her small body. When it seemed she could take no more, the spirit would exit the white-tail, laughing as it fled through the air. Andreena once again saw gentle Mother White-tail, but learned to dread her presence.

Andreena did not fear all creatures in the Realm of Rituals. There was Mother Robin, hopping through the grass, looking for food to feed her young babies. There were butterflies for Andreena to chase through the rays of sunlight that danced in the leaves. The butterflies sang as they played with Andreena, and they told her stories of how some day she would grow up to be as beautiful as a butterfly. They made her heart happy.

Andreena did not have much to be happy about. She lived in a castle in the Realm of Rituals. This was not a pretty castle like the ones she read about in fairy tales. It was dark and cold, with many frightening rooms.

Andreena was forever getting lost in the castle's maze of corridors. There were many days when she doubted that it was really her living in such a dismal place. There were no cozy rooms for a child to play in. The walls and floors were made of stone, and she often fell and bruised her knees. Her mother, the Queen, set many rules to follow, and in each room she assigned specific duties to Andreena. Then the Queen would change the rules, so Andreena made many mistakes.

The Queen put Andreena in charge of the Baby Room. Andreena hated that room. It was filled with crying babies and little children that she had to take care of. It was hard to keep them all quiet, but the Queen hated crying. Andreena's Fairy Grandmother helped her in that room. The Fairy Grandmother gave Andreena magical crayons so Andreena could color blankets that were warm and safe to wrap around each child. She colored clothes for the children to wear each day. She colored food for the children to eat. The Fairy Grandmother taught Andreena to sing comforting lullabies in her head so the Queen would not hear her.

Andreena cared for the children as best she could, but she could not save them from the Queen or the forest. Andreena would become tired at night and fall asleep, and then the Queen would come in and steal a child. Andreena was not as powerful as the Queen and could not stop her. But she had a secret that even the Queen did not know. When Andreena was out in the forest, in the Realm of Rituals, she could hear the children crying, and she would grab a child's soul out of the air and lock it inside her head. She gathered many of the lost children's souls that way. Andreena kept them hidden inside her body where no one could find them.

The children were thankful that Andreena had rescued them. They all helped her deal with the evil Mother Queen. They were the Little Ones of Andreena.

The Little Ones became Andreena's strength against the Queen. They helped Andreena's feet run faster when the Queen became angry and wanted to hit her. They helped Andreena stand tall when facing the King. They helped Andreena when she had to go into the forest at night. It was frightening there in the darkness, with all the night creatures out. The Little Ones were with her, and listened for danger.

The Little Ones helped Andreena in the Baby Room and in the other rooms. The rooms at the top of the stairs were the most difficult for Andreena. She was terrified of the steep, dark stairs. Trolls lived under them. Andreena tried to be very quiet when using the stairs so as not to waken the trolls. But they could always hear Andreena trembling and would lie in wait for her.

As Andreena climbed the stairs, holding her breath, a troll would reach out and grab her ankle. Sometimes they made her stumble; other times she would fall to the bottom. Andreena screamed for the Queen. The Queen would appear and become very angry. The Little Ones, longing for a loving mother, called her Mommy and wanted to be held. The Queen struck out instead. So the

Little Ones had to carry Andreena up the stairs.

At the top of the stairs were two guard trolls. They were as big as Andreena. They were very old, with wrinkled faces. They wore dirty, torn clothing. One of the trolls looked right at Andreena. His eyes could see all. She was afraid that he could see the Little Ones hiding inside her. She opened the door to run into the room, and one of the Little Ones came out and pushed the trolls down the stairs. Andreena felt as if she were turning into the evil Queen. She walked inside the room as she heard the trolls running after her.

Inside the room, candles burned, and there was an eerie glow. By the light of the glow, Andreena could see ghosts in the corners, staring at her. The floor creaked, and one of the ghosts walked toward her. Andreena shivered. She was afraid of the ghosts and their icy touch. The Little Ones came out as she was led into the circle of ghosts and placed on the table. Where was the Queen who had forced her here? Andreena was so frightened that the Little Ones took her on a journey away from that room.

They took her into the warm sunlight, where she was flying with the butterflies. There was no evil forest here. Andreena could hear her real mother calling. Just as she was about to reach her, Andreena awoke. She was in a puddle of black magic, with evil spirits dancing around her head. She screamed for her Fairy Godmother. The Godmother appeared in a white light and whisked Andreena away. They flew through the castle and over the Realm of Rituals, higher and higher until they reached the clouds. There the Fairy Godmother placed Andreena and the Little Ones on a cloud and wrapped her wings around them and rocked them to sleep.

The next morning, Andreena wakened to the sound of the Queen's thundering footsteps in the corridor. The Queen burst through the door with the King and two ghosts. The Queen pulled Andreena out of bed and threw her onto the cold stone floor. In the Queen's hands were what was left of the Fairy Godmother's wings. She handed each ghost one of the torn wings.

Andreena watched in horror as the ghosts swallowed her Fairy Godmother's wings. The Queen had killed the Fairy Godmother, and Andreena and the Little Ones could no longer be safe. Andreena was given to the King to be punished.

The King taught Andreena much about the Realm of Rituals. More than she ever wanted to know. He took her into the depths of the forest where everything smelled dead. Deeper and deeper into the forest she went. The trees whispered about her as she walked by. Some of them lashed out at her with their tough branches.

The ground was wet beneath her feet. She stepped on toads and felt their poison seep into her. The King forced her to go on.

At last they reached their destination. It was a circle of oaks. Andreena tried to climb one to hide. The oak grabbed her with his branches and threw her to the ground. The King laughed at her.

Ghosts were chanting with the frogs and crickets. The King was holding a magical sword, ready to kill the Little Ones. Andreena tried to save some of the children's souls floating in the air. They wouldn't come to her, for she too held a magical sword. She was becoming an Evil Princess. Andreena panicked. She had to run away, as far from the Realm of Rituals as she dared to venture. She had to abandon her Little Ones.

Deep into the forest she went. Andreena feared she would never find her way out. Yet on she pushed, struggling through vines and branches that caught at her hair. Just when she thought she could go no further and the forest would swallow her forever, she saw a tiny light. It was hardly a flicker, but to Andreena it looked like a beautiful glow.

She stumbled closer and saw that the light came from a window in a cottage. It was a candle, and it guided her footsteps on the path to the door. Timidly she knocked. An old woman, wrinkled and bent, opened the door. Andreena wanted to run away in fright, but the stranger's face looked kind, and she invited Andreena in with a gentle smile.

Inside, a fire burned in the hearth and a pot of nourishing stew simmered on the stove. The old woman offered Andreena a place at the table and said she was welcome to stay. "Here you are safe," she said. "You have much to learn, and I will teach you."

So began Andreena's lessons. At first she had no trust in the old woman. She waited for blows and angry rage. But they never came, and gradually she and the old woman became fast friends. The old woman's kindly, wise ways reminded Andreena of the Fairy Godmother the Queen had destroyed. Once or twice she was sure she spotted fuzzy, gauzy wings growing from the old woman's shoulders.

Andreena had been in the darkness for a long time. When she came to the cottage, she believed she was ugly and evil. But the old woman showed her new ways, and Andreena began to feel a light in her own face, reflecting the light and love in the old woman.

One day, while they were walking by a nearby stream, Andreena realized that she felt happy and strong. She looked at the animals and birds in the forest, and she smiled. They were no longer threatening. The two friends sat on a mossy log in their favorite clearing, and suddenly they heard children's voices. Peeping from behind each tree was a Little One! Andreena cried. She had missed them so and felt so guilty for abandoning them. With the old woman's encouragement, she beckoned them to her, one by one.

After that, whenever they entered the clearing, their special circle of magic, another Little One ventured out shyly and rested her head in Andreena's lap. After a long time, all the Little Ones had come into the magic circle. Some were still angry and hurt that Andreena had left them, and she had to listen with patience to their cries and tears. She felt calm now, and she could stroke their hair and tell them over and over that she loved them and would protect them.

One day the old woman gave Andreena a kiss on her cheek and said she was leaving, because Andreena was strong enough to care for the Little Ones alone.

Andreena wept. She was not ready to care for them alone! She raged! How could her benefactor leave her, abandon her like this! As she lay on the grass crying, she felt a tingling on her shoulders. At first she thought a beetle or a bee was resting there. She moved her hand to brush it away and touched something feathery and soft. It was the beginning of a wing.

She looked in surprise at her friend, who smiled and said, "You see, Andreena, fairy godmothers can never be destroyed. I have been here all the time. Now you have your center, Andreena. You are strong. You are healing. You have awakened from a bad dream of a lifetime, and you have the strength and wisdom to pull all the Little Ones into your center and live as a united family. Love them, guide them, and trust them, for each has a message for you."

With that, the Fairy Godmother floated away, her fuzzy wings fluttering. Andreena sat in the magic circle. She felt love and gratitude, and from that day on, she gave her Little Ones all that she had received. She was full of light now, and she saw that she could be a healer for others who had escaped from the Realm of Rituals.

Leaving the Land
of Shadows

Judy McDuffy

ong, long ago in the Land of Shadows, there lived a King and Queen. They had a beautiful daughter named Anna. The King kept Anna with him all the time. He loved to pet her and he talked very softly into her ear so no one else would know their secrets. Everyone admired the beautiful child and how the King loved her so.

The Queen grew very jealous of the attention the King gave to Anna and the admiration the people had for the two of them. She decided she wanted all of the admiration for herself. The Queen began to spy on the King and Anna until she discovered their secret. To punish the King, the Queen kept Anna and banished the King from the land forever.

The Queen ordered Anna to be beautifully dressed and groomed always. The Queen watched Anna's every move, making certain the child behaved properly at all times. Anna was not allowed to do anything without permission. The Queen basked in the admiration the people gave her for having such a marvelous daughter. But Anna was not happy.

Years passed, and instead of growing up, Anna became smaller and smaller. All the people who used to say what a wonderful child Anna was began asking what was wrong. Why did Anna seem so sad and why was she so small? The Queen was very angry. She ordered Anna to stop being sad and to stop getting smaller. The Knight, the Queen's vicious companion and protector, punished Anna for upsetting the Queen. Yet Anna continued to grow smaller. The Queen became angrier and the Knight became more cruel.

One day, when Anna had been ordered from the castle and was sitting on a rock in a grassy field, a mouse climbed on the rock beside her. "Why are you crying?" Mr. Mouse asked.

"Because I have been punished and I am all alone," she said.

"Well, dry your tears, Anna," Mr. Mouse said. "I know all about you, and I can help you. If you come with me to the Land of Fancy, I will love you and make you happy."

So Anna, who was very small by now, went with Mr. Mouse to the Land of Fancy. He gave her a mouse suit to wear and taught her how mice should behave. He explained how she should hold her ears a certain way and how she should eat so she would fit in with the mice in the Land of Fancy. She tried and tried, yet still she had trouble being accepted. The others knew she was different. As the years passed, she grew more and more unhappy and smaller and smaller.

One morning Anna could no longer wear the mouse suit. When the mice saw who she really was, they were horrified and angry and said she had tried to trick them. They turned their backs on her. Even her own children said she was not like them and they did not want her around ruining their lives.

Anna knew the time had come for her to leave. So she went by herself far into the forest. She wandered aimlessly among the trees, until she came upon a big, dark cave. Tired and heartsick, seeking safety and rest, she stepped into the cave and felt the darkness close around her as she walked to the very heart of the cave. There she lay down on a pile of leaves and fell into a deep, deep sleep.

Anna did not know that others were living in this immense cave. It was the home of a huge black bear and a spider. While Anna slept, Bear and Spider watched her and felt her sorrow and loneliness, and they decided to help her. With her great strength, Bear built a snug home for her. Spider spun fine thread and wove beautiful clothes for her. They both brought her tasty morsels of food.

When Anna awoke, Bear and Spider welcomed her with hearts full of love. Bear gathered her up into huge furry arms and snuggled and rocked her. Spider tenderly combed her hair. Anna glowed with the love and care she received.

Gradually, nourished by her new friends and safe in her cozy home, Anna grew well and strong, and she began to move toward the mouth of the cave, where she could see a glimmer of light. At last the day came when she stepped out of the cave. She was not afraid, because Bear and Spider were with her. They had promised to stay with her always. She was taller now, and she smiled more, filled with Bear's strength and the beauty of Spider's weaving.

Together they moved into the Land of Sunshine, where those who would harm her were frightened off by Bear and Spider, and those who approached in friendship were warmed by her glow.

The Wise One

Cheri Lee

The Indian maiden awakens and watches the sun rise. It has been a long, dark night, and she has been cold for a very long time. The warmth of the sun embraces her with its arms of fire. The colors talk to her, saying, "Trust me."

The Indian maiden looks about her and sees her favorite things: her cat, the colors of her room, her possessions, the deep greens of the trees and meadow outside, and the blue sky. She loves the silence of the morning, how clean and clear it is, and how unlike the confusion and noisy words of so many of her tribe.

In her tribe, women become who they are to be in midlife. She has forgotten her age, but feels deep inside that something important is happening. She has a sense of needing to go somewhere, but she does not know where. Something is waiting to be discovered in a place within. As she moves about in her home she feels safe.

She knows that everything she has learned and all her experiences, both sad and happy, can give her strength as she moves into a new place of becoming. And she knows she must let the past go if she is to be who she can be and fully live. Tears flow.

She hears music. She remembers being in the forest, feeling the energy and hearing the plants and trees talking to her. It was as if she had shifted to an animal presence and a connection with all living things, with a sense of complete peace and joy. The maiden understands that she must learn what her plant and animal brothers and sisters are trying to teach her, for they have much to share with humans.

The tears have stopped and peace fills her being. Now she knows she must explore the dark side.

She visits the wise old woman of her village. The old woman's wrinkled face brightens as the maiden approaches, for she knows it is her time. The wise one invites the maiden in. They sit in silence. The maiden is comfortable, appreciating the warmth and love. Her anxiety over her future fades and disappears.

After a long time, the wise one says, "Allow your knowledge to flow out."

The maiden replies, "I already do that."

The wise one looks sternly at the maiden and says, "Those are the talents you show the world, not your true knowledge. True knowledge is the gift of wisdom that you have accumulated throughout your lifetime. It is more than reciting what you know and have learned. You are tapping into a very deep part of yourself—a river of wisdom that you have hidden from the world until now. You must allow this river to flow from your innermost center and trust it. And you must share it with others, for you are entering your time of becoming. Be truthful to yourself, for you are the only one who knows your truth. Grieve no more for the past; it has no place in your future. You are who you are because of those who have caused you pain, those who have misunderstood you, those who have not seen the truth and beauty in you."

"How can I do this alone?" asks the maiden. "Who are my teachers? How can I change the world?"

The old woman's smile is patient. "It will not be easy to change what the outside world has done. You will have to fight for yourself. No one else can save you or find that lost part of yourself. But you can learn from the elder women who come across your path. They will guide you to the higher plain. For now, trust your inner knowing and look less to outer action. You are in a time of balancing your energies, and that deep river is moving up and through you."

As the maiden sits listening, it all makes sense to her. She gives her thanks and stands to leave, and so does the wise one. They embrace, and the wise one disappears.

The maiden leaves the wise one's dwelling and returns to her home. She surrounds herself with colors. She feels strength from the warmth and vibrancy of these colors. She envelops herself with the thought of her mate, knowing that all is well and he will not try to hold her back. At this moment of surrendering into peace, she feels the presence of the wise one but cannot see her. Suddenly the maiden realizes the wise one is in her.

As the maiden moves forward she hears, "Let

me live. I will love and guide you through our journey." So the maiden embarks on a new path knowing that only she can choose the path and shape it while she learns.

As the sun sets, she hears the words, "Trust me."

Seeds of Salvation

Jane Irvine

nce there was a land inhabited entirely by women. The women lived in a village in the forest, surrounded by the protective arms of great trees, a flowing stream, and soft mossy earth. Every day the women would leave the village and gather in the heart of the forest, quietly forming a ring around the Great Mother. The Great Mother was old and wise. She knew how to talk with the trees and the trees told her of all the mysteries of life. She taught the women how to listen, for she knew the time would soon come when they would need to remember and tell their stories.

The women's connection with the earth was so complete they could create life with their hands. They would dig deep into the soft brown earth, taking with it stones, moss, and leaves, heavy with moisture and compost. They gathered the soil into their hands, molding and forming it until a new life appeared. This life form was a child, composed of the earth and shaped deep in the minds and souls of the women.

A cold and bitter wind swept through the forest. For the first time, the women felt fear. The trees shook and trembled, and the women watched as the roots buckled the earth and the trees strained to stay erect. The women knew in their souls that the time had come. They gathered around the Great Mother and wept, for their intuition told them that the sweet dreamlike peace of their world was about to be destroyed.

One woman remained apart from the group. She knelt by the stream that flowed through the forest and began to create a life. Silently, quickly, she worked the clay soil, digging her hands into the muddy ball she formed. She was not afraid. As the trees began to crash upon the women's village, she kept working, for she knew that in her deft hands she held the key to survival. With a gentle breath, she blew life into the girl creature. Then the mother-creator disappeared.

The child lay by the stream bank, waiting.

Back in the village, the Great Mother raised her arms and encompassed the women in the loving folds of her body. She said, "I have nothing to tell you that you do not already know. You have what no one can take away. Listen, listen to your past, hear each other's stories."

She touched the women's abdomens, saying, "Here I have planted the seeds for your salvation. When the time is right, you will know." The Great Mother encapsulated herself in an egg and sank into the earth.

The conquerors came and turned the village into a fortress. They ripped out the trees, and the soil became barren. The women were in silent bondage. Some sprouted wings, took their souls, and flew away; others remained.

The child waited alone by the bank of the stream.

One day, as the child walked beside the stream, she came upon an old woman lying on the ground. The old woman was writhing in pain, her naked beauty turned to ugliness by self-loathing and hatred. As the child drew nearer, the old woman spat at her and warned, "Child, always remember you are dirt, dirt that heavy boots have trod upon." The child looked upon the old woman in amazement and fright. She did not know how to help. She remembered her mother's naked beauty, the soft folds of her body, the hands intent on creation.

The child stood by the bank of the stream, waiting.

Every day the twisted old woman would come and feed the child, leaving bits of bread upon the bank. The woman shrank from the child's eyes and whispered words of ill intent. The child longed to touch the shriveled fingers and thin legs covered with transparent skin that was cracked and dry. She longed to rub the old woman's skin, to make the pain go away, but she did not know how.

Years passed, and many hours of scanning the horizon, but the child still waited.

On a certain day, the child leaned over the stream to drink its cool water. In the depths of the stream she saw the eyes of her mother, watching her, and knew that she too had been waiting. "Mother, you have come," the child gasped in desperation. She scrambled to reach the water, longing for a drink. As the child's lips neared the surface, her breath made tiny ripples that spread the image across the water. She took great gulps and realized she was drinking in her own reflection.

The child waited no longer.

She grew stronger each day as she drank from the stream, knowing she was drinking her mother and her own reflection. She began taking buckets of the water to the women of the village. At first the women talked to the child in whispers, begging for stories, saying they knew of none. As time passed and as they drank the water, the women grew stronger and memories of the past spilled from their lips. The women gathered up their children and began to meet in the village under the trees that were left.

The conquerors were scared. They lashed out at the women, trying to stop them, but by now the women's force was so strong it could not be broken. The women remained unafraid and joined hands, listening to the call of their souls.

Not everyone came to the meetings. The old woman remained curled up in the hollow of a tree, silent. The child came to her and bent down. She dipped her hands into a bucket of stream water, cradling the contents in her palms, offering it to the old woman. The old woman's cracked lips parted and drank. The child touched the woman's shriveled hands, and the woman recoiled in shame. Gently, the child rubbed her knuckles and the palm of her hand, until relief flooded the old woman's face. She caressed the old woman's back and neck until her head rolled to the side and great tears streamed from her face. The child kissed her swollen eyelids and caressed her furrowed brow until her mouth hung open and great gasps of breath filled her lungs. Slowly the child massaged the shrunken belly until her howls of buried pain echoed throughout the remaining forest.

Hearing the old woman's cries, the women from the village came near. They drew her from the hollow of the tree. With the sunlight stinging her eyes, the old woman looked down and saw the wrinkled folds of her skin, the blue veins under the surface. She dipped her crooked fingers into the bucket of stream water and caressed her body. Her dry skin drank in the moisture, and for the first time the old woman realized she was beautiful. She remembered a woman of long ago who wore her aged skin with pride. The old woman traced with her fingers the dark spots marking her skin and remembered. She sat down upon the damp soil and spread her arms wide. The stories filled her mind and seeped from her lips. The women of the village drew their daughters nearer and caressed their swollen bellies with joy. They gathered around the old woman and listened. No one waited any longer.

So Good

Patricia Montgomery

nce upon a time, a little girl was born to a poor family on the edge of a big town. Times were very hard for them, and especially for the father who now had six other mouths to feed: his wife and five daughters. The little girl, named So Good, learned quickly how to stand out and be special: she was very, very good, and she smiled even when she was not happy. Neglected by her mother, So Good tried very hard to win her father's heart by doing everything he asked of her. She worked so hard she forgot how to play.

When So Good grew up, she wanted to find her Prince and live Happily Ever After. She met a beautiful golden Prince who put her under his spell. Charmed, she left the life that was familiar and moved far away to the Prince's estate in the hills.

There she was also charmed by the beautiful Queen, the Prince's mother. Young, naive, and trusting, So Good lived a happy life for many years. When nagging fears and doubts told her something was wrong, she pushed them aside and dedicated herself more strongly to state duties, her charming husband, and their children, the four young princes and the little princess. She pretended that she was very happy as a dutiful wife and daughter-in-law.

One day she had a dream, warning her of terrible things to befall her. Soon after, the Prince was stricken with a dreaded disease whose name was never to be mentioned. The Royal Family, especially the Queen, turned cold and harsh. So Good was banished to the outer edge of the estate, and the Prince spent his time at court with the Queen and King.

Remembering her dream, So Good decided to break the evil spell of the Queen and remove herself from her powers. Distraught as she realized that she would not live Happily Ever After and yet fearing for her own life and sanity, she ran far away, leaving her own children and the Royal Family. Besieged with guilt and loneliness, she began a new life in a new country. She worked diligently to achieve success, and she learned to slay dragons that threatened her.

A few years later, the Royal Queen and King died, and the Prince, now the King, finally managed to slay his dragon, the unnamed and dreaded disease. He went in search of So Good.

So Good and the Prince met again. They came together bathed in golden light, and they happily joined their lives once more. But after a while, So Good began to feel that she was falling into a deep, dark, bottomless pit. Confused and frightened, she went to a very wise woman and asked her what to do.

The wise woman told So Good that she must undergo an extremely difficult ordeal if she wished to destroy her final dragons. She would have to take a dark and dangerous trip that would endanger her body, mind, and spirit. So Good was terrified, but she knew she must take this journey alone. On her journey, she had to dive into her deepest girlhood memories, where she faced demons— shadowy, frightening figures that had stolen her light, joyful spirit and left behind an ugly burden of guilt and shame.

Courageously she fought the demons. She destroyed the fearsome burden and reclaimed her childhood innocence and beauty. She put on a magic ring her poor mother had given to her before she died, and with the help of its magic, she was able to see her mother in a different way. She could love and forgive her mother's failings.

In gratitude and humility, So Good returned with a new name: Peace. She was no longer worried about Happily Ever After, but lived each moment of each day. And that was enough.

Recommended Reading

Beck, Renee and Metrick, Sydney Barbara. *The Art of Ritual.* Berkeley: Celestial Arts, 1990.

Bolen, Jean Shinoda. *Goddesses in Everywoman: A New Psychology of Women.* San Francisco: Harper & Row, 1984.

Bridges, William. *Transitions: Making Sense of Life's Changes.* Reading, Mass: Addison-Wesley, 1980.

Campbell, Joseph. *The Power of Myth.* New York: Doubleday, 1988.

Chinen, Allan B. *Once Upon a Mid-life: Classic Stories and Mythic Tales to Illuminate the Middle Years.* Los Angeles: Jeremy P. Tarcher, 1992.

Christ, Carol P. *Diving Deep and Surfacing. Women Writers on Spiritual Quest.* Boston: Beacon Press, 1980.

Downing, Christine. *The Goddess: Mythological Images of the Feminine.* New York: Crossroads, 1981.

Eisler, Riane. *The Chalice and the Blade.* Cambridge: Harper Row, 1987.

Estés, Clarissa Pinkola. *Women Who Run with the Wolves.* New York: Ballantine Books, 1992.

Feinstein, David and Krippner, Stanley. *Personal Mythology, The Psychology of Your Evolving Self.* Los Angeles: Jeremy P. Tarcher, 1988.

Gimbutas, Marija. *The Goddesses and Gods of Old Europe, 6500 to 3500 BC, Myths and Cult Images.* Berkeley: University of California Press, 1982.

Hall, Nor. *The Moon and the Virgin: Reflections on the Archetypal Feminine.* New York: Harper & Row, 1980.

Iglehart, Hallie A. *Womanspirit: A Guide to Women's Wisdom.* San Francisco: Harper & Row, 1983.

Jung, Carl G. *Man and His Symbols.* Garden City, New Jersey: Doubleday, 1964.

Keen, Sam and Valley-Fox, Anne. *Your Mythic Journey.* Los Angeles: Jeremy P. Tarcher, 1973.

Kolbenschlag, Madonna. *Kiss Sleeping Beauty Goodbye: Breaking The Spell of Feminine Myths and Models.* San Francisco: Harper & Row, 1988.

Land, George and Jarman, Beth. *Breakpoint and Beyond: Mastering the Future—Today.* Champaign, Ill.: Harper Business, 1992.

Luke, Helen M. *Woman: Earth and Spirit: The Feminine in Symbol and Myth.* New York: Crossroads, 1981.

Monaghan, Patricia. *The Book of Goddesses and Heroines.* New York: Dutton, 1981.

Murdock, Maureen. *The Heroine's Journey.* Boston: Shambhala, 1990.

Nicholson, Shirley, compiler. *The Goddess Re-awakening: The Feminine Principle Today.* Wheaton, Illinois: Theosophical Publishing House, 1989.

Paladin, Lynda S. *Ceremonies for Change: Creating Personal Ritual to Heal Life's Hurts.* Walpole, New Hampshire: Stillpole, 1991.

Perera, Sylvia B. *Descent to the Goddess: A Way of Initiation for Women.* Toronto: Inner City, 1981.

Stein, Diane, editor. *The Goddess Celebrates: An Anthology of Women's Rituals.* Freedom, Calif.: Crossing Press, 1991.

Walker, Barbara G. *The Crone: Women of Age, Wisdom and Power.* San Francisco: Harper & Row, 1985.

Walker, Barbara G. *The Woman's Encyclopedia of Myths and Secrets.* San Francisco: Harper & Row, 1983.

Zweig, Connie, editor. *To Be a Woman: The Birth of the Conscious Feminine.* Los Angeles: Jeremy P. Tarcher, 1990.

About the Author

atricia Montgomery is in the forefront of teaching about women in midlife transition. She holds a master of science degree in education and a doctorate in East-West psychology. An organization development consultant as well as educator, she completed a graduate program in organizational development and transformation. Currently, she is a faculty member at Marylhurst College, offering classes on women and power, change, creativity, and mothers and daughters. Her thirty years of experience as an educator include Head Start, elementary, high school, and college teaching.

She offers retreats, seminars, and workshops on the psychological aspects of the change process. Her expertise is in helping people manage transitions creatively. She has done extensive research on women's midlife transition. Writing her dissertation on women making dramatic midlife career changes, she used in-depth interviews to research the transitions of six professional women.

She sees her mission as evoking transformational change in women that releases innate creativity and moves them to health and wholeness. Presently she is creating seminars to respond to the pressing need of women in spiritual crisis.

SIBYL PUBLICATIONS

Sibyl Publications is a small press of nonfiction books to empower women. Books are positive, calling forth women's strength and wisdom. We are dedicated to women's voices being heard.

Two New Books From Sibyl

MYTHMAKING: Heal Your Past, Claim Your Future
Patricia Montgomery, Ph.D.

Capture the power of myth by writing your life story in myth form. *MYTHMAKING* discusses the importance of telling your story and demonstrates with step-by-step instructions. Be inspired by 30 myths written by women in midlife. ISBN 0-9638327-3-5 $14.95

THE GODDESS SPEAKS: Myths & Meditations
Dee Poth

Evoke the wisdom of 25 ancient goddesses through this inspirational card set and book of stories about the goddesses. Colorful illustrations based on goddess images in museums around the world. 25 cards and 120-page book packaged together for daily use. ISBN 0-9638327-2-7 $29.95

Please send the following books:

_____
_____
_____
_____

To order books:

Phone orders: 1-800-240-8566 and have your VISA card ready.

FAX orders: (503) 235-8577

Mail orders: Sibyl Publications • 123 N.E. Third Avenue, #502 Portland, OR 97232-2972

Shipping: Add $2 for the first book and $1 for each additional book.

Please send me announcements of future books by Sibyl Publications:

Name _____
Address _____
City / State / Zip _____

Payment: ☐ Check ☐ VISA
Card Number: _____
Name on card: _____ Expiration date: _____
Signature: _____

Call 1-800-240-8566 toll free and order now